HOMEBREW WORLD

HOMEBREW WORLD

DISCOVER THE SECRETS OF THE WORLD'S LEADING HOMEBREWERS

Joshua M. Bernstein

STERLING EPICURE

New York

STERLING EPICURE
New York

An Imprint of Sterling Publishing Co., Inc.
1166 Avenue of the Americas
New York, NY 10036

The profile of Mary Izett appeared in different form, in "Getting Cultured," published by *Draft* magazine.
The profile of Jeff Mello appeared in different form, in "Counter Culture," also published by *Draft* magazine.
The profile of Phil Farrell appeared in different form, in "Party Fowl," published by *Imbibe* magazine.

ISBN 978-1-4549-2073-1

Distributed in Canada by Sterling Publishing Co., Inc.
c/o Canadian Manda Group, 664 Annette Street
Toronto, Ontario, M6S 2C8, Canada
Distributed in the United Kingdom by GMC Distribution Services
Castle Place, 166 High Street, Lewes, East Sussex, BN7 1XU, United Kingdom
Distributed in Australia by NewSouth Books
45 Beach Street, Coogee, NSW 2034, Australia

For information about custom editions, special sales,
and premium and corporate purchases, please contact
Sterling Special Sales at 800-805-5489
or specialsales@sterlingpublishing.com.

Manufactured in China

2 4 6 8 10 9 7 5 3 1

sterlingpublishing.com

Interior design by Christine Heun

A complete list of image credits appears on page 263.

TO ALL THE BREWERS
FERMENTING REVOLUTION
FIVE GALLONS AT A TIME

CONTENTS

Preface, viii

Introduction, xiv

PREFACE

n hindsight, it wasn't the smartest move to go on a beer tour by bike. It was 2008, and I felt bulletproof, no hangovers hitting like heavyweight right hooks, no toddler bouncing on my chest at 6 a.m. and making me rue last night's last call.

So Sean's and Clarissa's idea held real appeal. Sean White was president of the New York City Homebrewers Guild. We'd known each other since my undergrad days at Ohio University, a lifelong friendship cemented over long-necks of Schlitz. Like me, Sean had ended up in Brooklyn, where beer further infused both of our lives. I chronicled the lush life for *Imbibe*, *Gourmet*, *New York* magazine, *Time Out*, and outlets now relegated to history's recycling bin. Sean fell hard for homebrewing. His cramped apartment became a laboratory for Belgian tripels, witbiers, and other creations I readily consumed from his kegerator.

His beers were very good, the kind of good that led him, after a handful of hops and jumps, back to Athens, Ohio, to open Little Fish Brewing. But first, his then-girlfriend, now-wife, Clarissa, offered this brain flash: Wouldn't it be great to bike to homebrewers' homes across Brooklyn?

Yes, yes it would.

Sean arranged an itinerary. A dozen-odd folks signed on. We pedaled. We drank. We pedaled more. We drank more. Total strangers invited us into their homes, triggering the spine-tingling thrill of peeking into personal spaces. We saw proof positive that square footage posed no obstacle to making great beer. Who needed a garage or a backyard? These brewers were golden as long as they had a working stove and a closet.

When pedaling proved too much of a challenge, we swapped wheels for feet to finish the tour. At the end, I headed home happy, buzzed on good vibes. The homebrew tour had succeeded because of its unique mixture of voyeurism, inebriation, and education. That terrific triple threat lingered in my bones.

The following fall, New York City Beer Week organizers asked me to put together a tour. I devised several. The first featured my favorite scary dive bars. I had been a bar columnist for years, and dives fascinated me—namely why they frightened people. I wanted to show that scary-looking dives were actually the friendliest bars around, like sheep in wolves' clothing.

The second excursion was a homebrew tour. Taking inspiration from the bike tour with Sean and Clarissa, I thought it would be a blast to provide a looksee into the world of amateur brewers to discover what makes them tick and to show how limited space could serve as the crucible for the next great beer trend. The four-point tour included a barbecue pit stop and lasted nearly seven hours, leaving me drained and—let's be honest—fairly buzzed.

"When's the next tour?" people asked at the end.

Next tour? That was it!

But the more I thought about it, the more I realized that the tour had legs. I created another tour, then another, tapping into New York City's groundswell of brewing talent. We visited the Upper East Side apartment of Rich Buceta, who later founded SingleCut, then Basil Lee and Kevin Stafford in Brooklyn, years before they launched Finback.

My guidelines: three breweries per tour, four hours total, never the same tour twice. My tours went to all five boroughs by subway, bus, foot, and, on one memorable

stop to Roosevelt Island, by tram. Attendees arrived, timid and tittering, but beer soon lubricated the wheels of conversation, and the last stop often devolved into an impromptu house party. Tour-takers congregated in the kitchen and toasted. Strangers departed as fast friends.

I took the tours on the road to Portland, Maine, and Chicago, discovering dynamic amateur beer scenes wherever I traveled, which sparked the creation of this book. *Homebrew World* provides an all-access pass to some of the world's best homebrewers. Japanese law forbids brewing batches above 1% ABV, so what do homebrewers there do? It's against the law to homebrew at all in Thailand, yet the scene there is thriving. How do Thai homebrewers skirt the law? What challenges face brewers in the Nevada desert? Costa Rica? Israel? It turns out that they all have a lot in common. Languages and cultures differ, yes. Access to hops, grains, and yeast strains fluctuates from country to country, true, but every homebrewer speaks the lingo of creativity. Homebrewing is a delicious act of drinking disobedience, refuting the fermented status quo in order to fashion new flavors and take beer in unexpected new directions, just gallons at a time.

So let's punch your drinking passport and get started.

FUN FACT

Many homebrewers have graduated from my tours and events to become professional brewers or open their own breweries:

Anthony Accardi and Rob Kolb, Transmitter Brewing, Long Island City, NYC

Tony Bellis, Zack Kinney, and Pete Lengyel, Kings County Brewers Collective, Brooklyn, NYC

Bill Boguski and Craig Dilger, Foulmouthed Brewing, South Portland, Maine

Rich Buceta, SingleCut Beersmiths, Astoria, NYC

Jon Conner, Conner Fields Brewing, Grants Pass, Oregon

Chris Cuzme, Fifth Hammer Brewing, Long Island City, NYC

Eric Feldman and Marshall Thompson, Braven Brewing, Brooklyn, NYC (contract brewing)

Philip Gardner, Sean Torres, and Patrick Wade, Kills Boro Brewing, Staten Island, NYC

Basil Lee and Kevin Stafford, Finback Brewery, Glendale, NYC

Katarina Martinez, Lineup Brewing, Brooklyn, NYC

BJ Pichman, Forbidden Root Restaurant & Brewery, Chicago, Illinois

Jason Sahler, Strong Rope Brewery, Brooklyn, NYC

Merlin Ward, Wartega Brewing, Brooklyn, NYC

INTRODUCTION

Here's my open secret: I've never been much of a homebrewer. This may strike you as odd, heretical even. After all, why should you read a brewing book if I don't have a brew kettle, much less a freezer full of rare hops?

Well, I'm no neophyte. I've brewed with more proficient pals, stirred grains, added hops, bathed in steam, and cleaned, cleaned, cleaned until the stainless steel gleamed. The transformation of sugar water into happy hour—liquid alchemy with a sprinkle of razzle-dazzle—awes me. My days usually consist of clickety-clacking about beer on my computer, chased by evenings sampling beer and, more often than not, visiting a bar or brewery to drink more beer or attending an event where the focus is—*wait for it*—beer. The research is endless. But, no, I don't brew.

"*Really?*" many say, as if my beer-journalist DNA is missing some essential gene. The hobby is so accessible to so many, so why wouldn't I? The assumption is a rarity among alcohol writers, however. Wine reviewers don't stomp grapes regularly, nor do bourbon experts patiently age corn distillate in their basements.

Instead, my homebrew bona fides lie in deep, abiding fandom. I've become one of homebrewing's biggest boosters, a believer in the power of bringing strangers inside amateur brewers' homes and tapping homebrewers to pour at festivals. These simple actions literally give beer a friendly face. Brewers aren't faceless cogs slaving in some far-off factory. They're friends, colleagues, neighbors, spouses, significant others, folks who generously share both their knowledge and their beer.

"We're at the peak of popularity in homebrewing in America," says Gary Glass, director of the American Homebrewers Association. America has more than 1 million homebrewers, he notes, of which some 46,000 belong to his organization—and U.S. brewers have it relatively easy. Access to pristine ingredients and effective information lies merely a click away.

Brewers elsewhere ride a rockier road. In South America, Glass says, homebrewers essentially lack access to liquid malt extract, while Thai brewers have a tough time sourcing fresh hops. Then there's the language barrier: "Information for homebrewers comes from the United States," Glass says, noting the challenge of translating beer content. "There are a lot of German words and English words that don't translate, like *pale ale*."

Despite the difficulties, homebrew scenes are ascendant across Latin America, especially Argentina, Brazil, and Chile. Homebrewing has entrenched itself firmly in South Africa, New Zealand, and Australia, and Europe is fast finding its amateur footing.

It's easy to lean on tired old tropes, like the one about the bearded dude making beer in his basement, but today's homebrewers crush clichés like aluminum cans, overcoming limitations at every turn.

On an island outside Bangkok, Wichit Saiklao is training an army of homebrewers determined to rattle Thailand from its cold-lager lethargy. Denny Neilson immigrated from Tennessee to Israel and opened the nation's first homebrew shop, igniting the country's modern beer craze. In Iceland, six longtime friends repurposed a decades-old washing machine into a brewing system, importing brewing ingredients from Belgium to feed their hobby. Caleb Selby started an underground brewery in Suzhou, China, selling

California commons and pilsners to thirsty expats via social media. Mitch Grittman of New Orleans devises recipes for Smoothie King by day and wild and sour ales by night and weekend.

Nearly 40 years ago, Ken Grossman's early batches of Sierra Nevada Pale Ale broke new ground, the hoppy repercussions still reverberating even today. Tomorrow's next Earth-shattering beer is out there somewhere, maybe bubbling away in someone's basement in Patagonia or hanging out on a Hong Kong rooftop. Strategies, styles, and ingredients may differ from brewer to brewer, but these people share an unparalleled ability to turn the ordinary into something extraordinary.

"The homebrew community is the tip of the sphere," says Rob Widmer, cofounder of Widmer Brothers. "What they are doing now is what people will be drinking four or five years from now."

. . .

Writing a book isn't like assembling a high school yearbook, which includes everybody. At present, the world has 196 countries, and not every nation made the cut. (Sorry, Armenia, Bhutan, Yemen, and Zimbabwe!) My goal was to create a global snapshot of this moment in modern homebrewing, the makers' stories as important as where they're working their magic. Thus, brewers appear alphabetically in four broad categories: The Stylists nail tradition with time-honored styles such as the hefeweizen, porter, and mild. The Hop Pack boldly pushes IPAs and other hop-forward styles into fragrant new directions. The Funky Bunch harvest ambient yeast, unleash rowdy microbes, and muck about with sour-ing bacteria to extend the boundaries of good taste. The Creative Front follows only one rule. There are no rules.

Now let's see what they've got.

THE STYLISTS

These brewers crush classic styles with medal-winning precision.

WE WALK BEFORE WE RUN, AND homebrewers rarely zip from beer kits to nailing double IPAs with peaches and feral yeast. They have to master the basics first, refining their techniques, before their recipes can skitter off on wild tangents. Conquering the classics, the world's great pilsners and saisons, should come first. In the modern brewing world—where excess and novelty equal exultation—that mission often holds all the appeal of a doctor's visit. Put another way: Would you rather crank up Bach or the latest chart-topping banger?

Belgian tripels, English milds, and German hefeweizens have withstood changing moods and fickle fads. They define the brewing canon. The template for porters and pilsners stands firm, but there's ample wiggle room for experimentation. Think of brewing like a language: Why learn only a few words when you can have an entire avenue of expression? Here, we'll meet homebrewers who color neatly within the lines: meticulous Germans, Belgian-obsessed Brazilians, and San Diego casino workers who find perfection within parameters.

CHRISTOPHER BOURDAGES

BOWMANVILLE, ONTARIO

Chris Bourdages used to make some pretty crappy beer. A broke university student with a microbiology background aiming to shave a few bucks off his beer budget, he brewed with can kits, paying no mind to sanitation or temperature control. "I figured I'd give it the ol' college try," he says.

His batches improved incrementally, however, from drain pours to decent, from junky kits to stovetop-cooking partial mashes (which mixes extracts and grains). Even a sloth could applaud his growth rate. Homebrew clubs were scarce around Toronto at the time, so YouTube and Google mentored him. "There was zero community back then. I was the guy who started my community."

He founded Durham Homebrewers and started teaching people how to brew. An amateur instructing other amateurs may sound odd, but the club put Bourdages on a path of self-improvement by testing the limits of his burgeoning talents. Before the club's ninth meeting, he fashioned a rig with a camping cooler, brewing his inaugural all-grain beer. "It actually turned out pretty darn good. I served that at the meeting and also showed other members how to brew all-grain. I wanted to keep everybody ahead of the game."

Like many, he quickly fell under IPA's spell, brewing double this and imperial that. "You taste something that's a little hoppy, and you're like, *Ooh, there's flavor*. But you get sick of IPAs. You get sick of hoppiness. You want to explore different flavors and profiles."

The Beer Judge Certification Program's style guidelines delineated a flavorful constellation of pilsners, Scottish ales, fruit beers, and bocks, each category encircled by rigid parameters. One by one, Bourdages deeply researched each beer style, aiming to produce pinpoint representations, his eyes forever on the competition prize. "I medaled and got gold in every single BJCP category." His medal collection would make Michael Phelps jealous.

He won Canada's national title in 2014, nimbly knocking out double IPAs, Scotch ales, Belgian strong ales, dark lagers, and plenty of British porters and stouts. ("Lake Ontario has a salt profile that's very similar to London," he says.) He brews any and every style on his humble setup: a couple of tailgate coolers, a keg custom-converted into a kettle, and a corny keg for fermenting. "Everything is DIY. If I build it, I can also troubleshoot and fix it if anything ever breaks."

This is normally the point in the story where a brewer's professional aspirations take over. "When you lose the passion and you lose the drive, then it becomes work. That's why I'm always afraid of turning it into a profession." For the moment, the registered nurse is contently keeping his brewing pursuits personal. He grows Cascade and Nugget hops in his backyard and patiently oversees a sour program in his basement. Having won Canada's top honors, he decided to mess with mead, wine, and cider, and he grabbed the Canadian cidermaker of the year title with his first ferment.

His homebrew club has swelled to some five hundred members, and the communal aspect explains his attraction to the hobby. Novices receive hands-on instruction and advice backed by years of experience, which allows newbies to hit the stove running. "When they bring me their beer, it's often fantastic. When there's a community involved, the growth curve is so much greater. It's very therapeutic, creating something from nothing, and then being able to share it with others is rewarding."

ADVICE

- "Break free from your drinking comfort zone to find new inspiration. Go to your local liquor stores and try a bunch of different styles that you've never tried."

- "Solid fermentation distinguishes a good beer from an absolutely fantastic beer. It's all about yeast viability, adequate pitching rates, temperature control, oxygenation saturation, and sanitation. It's funny that many brewers will spend thousands of dollars on brewing rigs and very little on the cold side. I always encourage new brewers to invest in a temperature controller and a fermentation chamber rather than buying a fancy new brew pot."

BREWER SPOTLIGHT

Members of the Durham Homebrewers club later founded Ontario's Five Paddles Brewing (try the Home Sweet Home honey-vanilla wheat ale) and IPA-focused Manantler Craft Brewing.

50 POINT MILD
English Mild
CHRISTOPHER BOURDAGES

"This beer is a real winner! It's my only beer to receive a perfect BJCP score of 50 (a mysterious and elusive unicorn said to be wholly unattainable by mortal men). Thanks to mild malt, this beer drinks like a cross between a rich northern English brown and an extra special bitter. It's fantastic for those who want to slake their thirst without getting too wobbly. Raise a pint and toast the sacred unicorn you now hold firmly in your grasp."

SIZE	5 gallons (18.9 L)
ORIGINAL GRAVITY	1.032
FINAL GRAVITY	1.007
IBU	15
SRM	17
ABV	3.2%

MALTS AND ADJUNCTS
4.5 pounds (2.04 kg) Mild Malt
8 ounces (0.23 kg) Pale Chocolate
6 ounces (0.17 kg) Caramel/Crystal Malt
4 ounces (0.11 kg) Caramel/Crystal Malt

HOPS (60-MINUTE BOIL)
0.75 ounce (21 g) East Kent Golding (5% AA), 60 minutes

YEAST
1 package Lallemand Danstar Windsor Ale Dry Yeast

NOTES
Mash Mash temperature, 152°F (67°C), 60 minutes
Sparge temperature, 168°F (76°C)

NICK CORONA

Nick Corona grew up in Carlsbad, near San Diego, the city of endless sun and IPAs, but he never cared much about beer. It offered a cold, bubbly means to an end. That changed one night, though, when a buddy offered him an Avery Maharaja, a pungent imperial IPA packing a 10% ABV wallop.

"Each sip was liquid gold," he says. "I kept having a sip and another sip, and the beer changed with every sip. It was absolutely enjoyable." One Maharaja led to three, so a friend drove Corona home. When he awoke the next morning, he had a black eye and abrasions on his right hand. He pieced together what happened: As he walked in, his head collided with a doorjamb. In response, he punched the door.

"The first things that went through my mind were: *Somebody made that beer, and I want to make that beer.*" He resolved to order a homebrew kit and open a brewery. "I wanted to give someone the experience that I was given."

Corona found the Maharaja recipe online and set out to replicate it. "Obviously, it wasn't easy. My first eight to ten beers were IPAs. Of those, I made only one that was decent." Undaunted, he kept brewing, his breakthrough coming with a fourth-place finish for his hefeweizen at the San Diego County Fair. "The awards go to fifth place. Thank goodness I was able to see I was somewhat close. I decided I'd hold on to that recipe and continue to brew it."

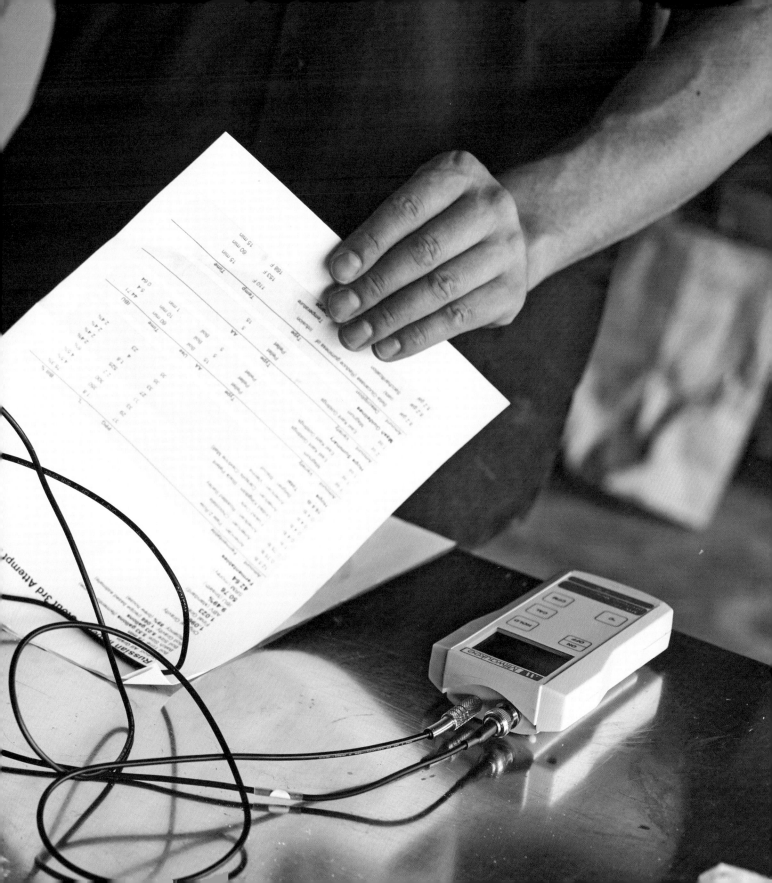

Therein lies the secret to Corona's success: repetition. He settled on a style—be it stout, lager, or coffee beer infused with whole beans—and polished the recipe until it was flawless. Before brewing: "Research, research, research. I'll put together my calculations on a recipe and go back and recalculate and recalculate again."

He craves constructive criticism now because he rarely received feedback during his early brewing days. He often took growlers to softball games and poured cups for his pals. "They'd sit there and say they liked it, but I didn't see many people going back for second cups. Their cups would sit there halfway full for some time. When those cups started getting emptier, that's when I realized they were telling me the truth." His hard work paid dividends on the awards dais, earning him best of show at the prestigious Mayfaire Homebrew Competition in 2015, organized by the long-running Maltose Falcons club. "That's when I started to build up confidence that maybe I can do this."

Corona's coronation came during the 2016 National Homebrew Competition. He won gold for his German wheat, and judges named him America's homebrewer of the year. "To hear your name announced on homebrewing's biggest stage was mind-blowing."

With the blessing of his wife, Kandy, he's turned a garage bay into his brewing lair, outfitting it with chest freezers and a stainless steel Brutus 10 stand. He has fifteen-gallon More Beer kettles, but he rarely brews more than five gallons at a time. He bottles most of his beer and earmarks the lion's share of it for competitions. For him, the feedback is more important than growlers for friends. "I really enjoy competition brewing, and I want to get unbiased opinions. You don't want to put all this time and effort into something and feel that it's being torn apart, but you really need that to improve."

Still, Corona is eyeing the next level. "The reason I got into brewing wasn't just to make beer for myself. One day I hope to make a beer that changes someone from buying 50-cent cans of Miller Lite to seeking out one of my beers at a bottle shop."

ADVICE

"Reach out to people for help. There's no big secret in the homebrew community. At the same time, it's important, when you first start, to brew the same recipe. Ask someone you trust, 'What's a good recipe to start with?' If you brew it over and over, you'll find that you're not necessarily perfecting that recipe, you're perfecting that process. Most of the problems I had were not with recipes but with my process."

BREWER SPOTLIGHT

Widmer Brothers' landmark unfiltered Hefeweizen originated with founding brothers Rob and Kurt Widmer's early homebrew experiments. They released the beer in 1986, but Rob is still tinkering with the recipe on a one-gallon kit. "People are like, 'Oh god, how boring is that? Haven't you figured that out?' " Rob says. "It reminds me of the infinite variability of brewing on that scale. It reminded me how simple the process is. I don't really need a volume. I'm awash in beer. I want to jump in, smell the smells, and start the process again."

BARB'S HEF
Hefeweizen
NICK CORONA

"Outside of requiring a system that allows a step mash, this is a relatively easy brew. When I brewed this beer at Hangar 24, their system didn't allow for a step mash. We were able to do a two-part infusion and skip the protein rest. The first rest produces ferulic acid, necessary for the yeast to produce the style's clove-like phenols. Banana esters can come across as a banana bomb or even bubblegum, so I control this through restrained fermentation temperatures during the first few days. Brewers looking to perfect this style should closely monitor the initial stages of fermentation."

SIZE	5 gallons (18.9 L)
ORIGINAL GRAVITY	1.046
FINAL GRAVITY	1.009
IBU	15.2
SRM	3.6
ABV	4.8%

MALTS AND ADJUNCTS
4.5 pounds (2.04 kg) German Pilsner
4.5 pounds (2.04 kg) White Wheat Malt
0.5 pound (0.23 kg) Rice Hulls

HOPS (90-MINUTE BOIL)
0.25 ounce (7 g) Hallertau Mittelfrueh (3% AA), 90 minutes
0.75 ounce (21 g) Hallertau Mittelfrueh, 30 minutes

YEAST
2 packages (1.5 L starter) White Labs WLP 380 Hefeweizen IV Ale

NOTES
Mash Add 1⅓ teaspoons (6.5 g) calcium chloride to mash.
Ferulic Acid Rest, 115°F (46°C), 10 minutes
Protein Rest, 127°F (53°C), 10 minutes
Mash temperature, 149°F (65°C), 60 minutes

Brewing Add ⅔ teaspoon (3.4 g) Diammonium phosphate with 10 minutes left in the boil.

Fermenting Ferment at 66–70°F (19–21°C).

Post-fermentation Carbonate to 3.5 volumes CO_2.

PHIL FARRELL

CUMMING, GEORGIA

f you've been to one of America's hallmark beer fests—the Great American Beer Festival or the Oregon Brewers Festival—you might've met Phil Farrell, aka the Chicken Man. When he spots someone he deems picture-worthy (Stone Brewing's Greg Koch, Lost Abbey brewmaster Tomme Arthur, Alaskan Brewing's Geoff Larson), he thrusts a rubber chicken into his mark's hand, brandishes a camera, and, on the count of three, they've entered the Chicken Man's digital scrapbook of more than ten thousand photos. "Sometimes people look at me like, *What are you doing?* I'm like, 'I need your mojo for the chicken.' I try to have fun with beer."

His beer interest stemmed from flight. In the 1970s, he enrolled in the Air Force Academy, which took him around the globe. Each stop offered an opportunity to sample curiosity-sparking brews. "I wondered, *Why does English beer taste different than German, Belgian, or American beer?*" His interests gradually shifted from drinking to brewing, and nearly 30 years ago his wife bought him a homebrew kit for Christmas. Broadband Internet didn't exist yet, and homebrew shops were still rare in the DIY desert.

"When I started homebrewing, you couldn't just roll into a homebrew shop. There were not a lot of people with knowledge." He started with a solitary pot on his stove and extract ingredients, the equivalent of a cook making meals on a single burner. "It was a way to learn the process," but extract beer has an excellence limit. "After I'd done multiple batches and the beer was good, it was basically as good as the ingredients would allow." He joined a homebrew club, discovering the multiple pathways to making beer, chiefly the ingredients. "The only way to make better beer was to go all-grain and use fresh hops."

He began with IPAs before trying stouts, English ales, and German lagers. "I'd do a couple of batches and try to do it better each time." His perfectionism resulted in ribbons, trophies, and medals stacked like week-old newspapers. "I stopped counting after five hundred." He filled his basement with brewing ephemera—coasters, glasses, hats, jackets, mirrors, neon signage—and his fridges with beer cooked on a rolling brewing system custom-built from stainless steel kegs, valves, propane burners, and temperature gauges. "I came up with the half-barrel brewery using converted kegs. It was portable without being overly crazy and complicated."

Farrell learned the ins and outs by repeatedly brewing all-grain batches with experienced brewers. "Find somebody who brews good beer, pay for the ingredients, split a batch, and drink the beer. You realize, *I can do this well if I follow these steps.*"

Over the years, Farrell has fancied up his system, his equipment evolving in lockstep with his skills. "I can go to a beer joint, look at the taps, and go, 'Yeah, I can make that, that, that, and that.' Sometimes I do that just for fun." His brews are remarkable for being unremarkable because he aims to imitate professional beers in their consistency and quality. "Nobody would drink it and say it's anything other than a commercial offering," he says

of beers such as his pale ale, often mistaken for Sierra Nevada's landmark version.

Few people have more fun with beer than Farrell. Over three decades, the Delta pilot has sipped brews in every European country—including Vatican City—the Philippines, and even Diego Garcia, a pipsqueak island in the Indian Ocean. Domestically, he and his wife, Suzie, crisscross the country in their RV, hitting America's bars, breweries, and beer festivals. A grand master in the Beer Judge Certification Program, he judges brewing competitions across the Americas, sharing tricks he's gleaned as an award-winning homebrewer. "Judging, making beer, drinking beer, they're all different skillsets, but I'm really good at tasting things and coming up with ideas. I'm good at deconstructing beers in my mind. What's the signature here? Well, it's the spiciness, the fruitiness, the maltiness. There's always something that stands out."

Neither his pilot career nor his zest for beer is diminishing anytime soon. Charlie Papazian inaugurated Farrell's fourth chicken, the latest versions made from vinyl instead of latex. "They don't make chickens the way they used to," Farrell laments. But he continues to serve as a vice president of the Beer Judge Certification Program, and he sits on the Board of Governors of the American Homebrewers Association. "In other words, I have a lot of people fooled."

FUN FACT

Homebrew Con, organized by the American Home-brewers Association, attracts thousands to the annual three-day gala and features seminars, demonstrations, and so, so, so much beer.

ADVICE

- "Have fun. Don't take it too seriously. Don't set high goals for yourself. You can't get a beer kit and say, 'I'm going to make the best beer in the history of the world.' That's setting yourself up for failure. You are going to be so disappointed. I'm not Nostradamus, but I can predict that you won't make the best beer."

- "Unless you own a brewery, you don't have to please anybody but yourself. Impress yourself first. If you have a solid recipe and your fermentation is sound and you don't add any infection sites, you'll have no problem."

- "It's important for new brewers or people who are thinking about brewing to realize that you can use plastic buckets and bottles with repurposed kitchen items to make beer—just like you can start entry-level cooking with a little electric hot plate. I accumulated my equipment over 20 years."

- "Pre-fermented wort that's already chilled is like asking for an infection. The longer you wait to pitch yeast, the more likely something bad is going to happen."

MAD COW XXX MILK STOUT II
PHIL FARRELL

"This is the original recipe for Mad Cow XXX Milk Stout. It says 'II,' but I did so well on the first one I didn't change anything, I only added to my notes. The inspiration was Mackeson XXX. I wanted something bigger and bolder without noticeable alcohol. I have modified and done variations on the basic recipe many times, scaling it up into an Imperial Milk or even an Imperial Stout as well as taking it down a notch to make it more of a session beer. The hops and yeast are English. This beer isn't about the hops or the yeast; it's about the malt and the roast. I can't emphasize enough, however, that the English ingredients add a nuance that I like. This is a kitchen sink–type grain bill that homebrewers are famous for, especially from the early 2000s. There're nuttiness, coffee, chocolate, and even an espresso-with-cream nuance that my wife likes. The flaked rye adds a touch of spiciness, while there are caramel and a complex oatmeal texture. The mouthfeel on soft carbonation or nitro is wonderful."

SIZE	5 gallons (18.9 L)
ORIGINAL GRAVITY	1.075 (1.069 before lactose)
FINAL GRAVITY	1.023
IBU	38.3
SRM	55.6
ABV	6%

MALTS AND ADJUNCTS

6.5 pounds (2.95 kg) English Pale Malt (2-Row) (3°L)

1.5 pounds (0.68 kg) Crystal 60L (60°L)

1 pound (0.45 kg) Briess CaraPils (2°L)

1 pound (0.45 kg) Chocolate Malt (350°L)

1 pound (0.45 kg) Wheat Malt (2°L)

0.5 pound (0.23 kg) Flaked Oats (2°L)

0.5 pound (0.23 kg) Flaked Rye (2°L)

0.5 pound (0.23 kg) Roasted Barley (575°L)

0.37 pound (0.17 kg) Black Malt (600°L)

1 pound (0.45 kg) Lactose

HOPS (90-MINUTE BOIL)

0.5 ounce (14 g) Wye Target (10% AA), 75 minutes

0.65 ounce (16 g) East Kent Golding (5% AA), 60 minutes

0.5 ounce (14 g) East Kent Golding, 15 minutes

YEAST

1 package White Labs WLP002 English Ale Yeast

NOTES

Mash Mash temperature, 152°F (66°C), 90 minutes

Mash out temperature, 167°F (75°C), 30 minutes

Sparge temperature, 170°F (77°C)

Brewing Add lactose with 30 minutes left in the boil. Add 1 unit Whirlfloc with 15 minutes left in the boil.

RONALDO DUTRA FERREIRA

ARMADA CERVEJEIRA
FLORIANÓPOLIS, BRAZIL
armadacervejeira.com.br

In 2009, Ronaldo Dutra Ferreira worked as a lawyer for a power company and homebrewing know-how was in short supply in Brazil. In his spare time, he cooked up everything from French cuisine to traditional Brazilian barbecue. Cooking steaks led to simmering malts and ordering instructional books from the Internet. He couldn't find any Portuguese guides, but Ferreira speaks English fluently. "My father is a university professor. Studying and reading have always followed me and been in my blood."

He bought malt and hops from a local brewing supplier who sold stock to homebrewers on the side. Another connection regularly traveled to America and muled back high-quality liquid yeast. Hard-to-find Belgian styles became Ferreira's first and lasting muse, and awards for them arrived as regularly as the mail. Ferreira invited beer experts such as Rare Barrel sour maestro Jay Goodwin to Brazil, shotgunning the scene with a hit of knowledge.

Winning Cervejeiria Bierland's 2012 homebrewing contest put a huge feather in Ferreira's cap. He had been brewing for only a handful of years, and the victory gave him the chance to collaborate with Bierland on a limited-edition batch of his Belgian-inspired strong blonde, Bruxa ("witch"). The unfiltered ale flaunted a bewitching banana fragrance, spicy bitterness, and a finish as dry

as the day is long. The judges at the 2013 World Beer Awards wrapped a silver medal around its neck. Not too shabby for a recipe made with cobbled-together valves and fittings, a mishmash of hardware-store parts, and equipment bought from America. "It was much more like a cooking device."

Going pro never piqued his interest, though. Ferreira had a great job—until he didn't. His firm went through a stormy patch, and his future looked as cloudy as a New England IPA. At the same time, he partnered in a local start-up brewery, which offered him a perfect opportunity to jump ship and switch careers. "Everything happened very naturally."

Unika operates in the mountainous town of Rancho Queimado, near Florianópolis, and features dual brands. Half the brewery makes German and American beers, such as Märzens and IPAs, while Bruxa, now a full-fledged brand, focuses on Ferreira's favored Belgians: dark saisons, strapping tripels, and blondes flavored with mixed fruit.

The members of Armada Cervejeira, his old homebrew club, used to meet every two weeks to discuss all things homebrew and taste amateur and commercial beers. He and his friends transformed the club into a collaborative brewery outfitted with 21 taps, pouring everything from rustic grisettes to fruited sours. "We can brew whatever we feel like and enjoy the results with our loyal customers." He also runs the Brazilian National Homebrew Conference, bringing American amateur-beer luminaries such as Stan Hieronymus and John Palmer to Brazil, and advocates for the translation of homebrew books into his native language. "I'm not too shy to pick up a phone and call people. I will do everything and anything possible to get knowledge."

Ferreira sees a bright future for Brazil's homebrew scene, from which native beers are emerging organically. It's rising from the ground up, not built with huge injections from investors' wallets. "We're not trying to create a style because it's not something that can be forced. We are trying to build some identity to what we're doing. We're going to see Brazil shine a little bit more on the world's beer scene."

ADVICE

"Participate in homebrewing clubs, subscribe to magazines, buy books, and study, study, study! You can never have too much information. The focus [at Armada Cervejeira] was learning and to increase the learning curve by sharing information."

BRUXA BELGIAN BLONDE ALE
RONALDO DUTRA FERREIRA

"I developed this Belgian blonde ale with my friend Rodrigo Tasca and won the Brazilian brewery Bierland's homebrew competition. This is the recipe that won the competition. Bruxa is a moderate-strength golden ale with high drinkability, a sweet and fruity aroma, and a dry finish."

SIZE	5 gallons (18.9 L)
ORIGINAL GRAVITY	1.067
FINAL GRAVITY	1.012
IBU	28
SRM	5
ABV	7%

MALTS AND ADJUNCTS
5.3 pounds (2.4 kg) Castle Château Pilsen Malt (1.8°L)
5.3 pounds (2.4 kg) Castle Château Vienna Malt (3°L)
4 ounces (110 g) Castle Château Acid Malt (3°L)
3.5 ounces (99 g) Castle Château Abbey Malt (17°L)
1.1 pounds (500 g) Demerara/Cane Sugar

HOPS (60-MINUTE BOIL)
1¾ ounces (50 g) East Kent Golding (5% AA) 60 minutes

YEAST
2 packages Wyeast 1214 Belgian Abbey Style Ale

NOTES
Water Profile (ppm) Adjust water to Ca: 90, Mg: 10, Na: 35, Cl: 60, SO4: 60

Mash Mash temperature, 151°F (66°C), 60 minutes
Mash out temperature, 158°F (70°C), 15 minutes

Brewing Add Demerara sugar with 15 minutes left in the boil. Add 0.5 teaspoon (2.2 g) yeast nutrient with 15 minutes left in the boil. Cool wort to around 70°F (21°C).

Fermenting Ferment at 65°F (20°C) for 3 days, then turn off temperature control for 7-10 days. Do not let the temperature go above 79°F (26°C).

Post-fermentation Cold crash at 32°F (0°C) for 1 week.

TOMASZ KOPYRA

○

OBORNIKI ŚLĄSKIE, POLAND

blog.kopyra.com

Poland's beer scene was barely smoldering at the dawn of the new millennium. Cookie-cutter lagers reigned. Variety meant the odd Baltic porter. "There were no hefeweizens, no schwarzbiers; there was nothing," says Tomasz Kopyra. He began making wine at home before trying his hand at brewing. It was 2004, just a couple of years after the country's first homebrew shop opened. "In Poland, the homebrew revolution was the beginning of the brewing revolution."

FUN FACT

One of Poland's most popular beer styles is the strong and rich Baltic porter, celebrated every January during Baltic Porter Day. Żywiec Porter is a widely available example.

Kopyra managed his father's supermarket and restaurant, eventually planning to take the reins. But brewing, blogging, then vlogging ("Talking about beer is easier than writing about it") gradually consumed his life. Since then he has become a voluminous beer vlogger and to date has recorded more than 2,000 YouTube videos, a collection of instructional style guides, impassioned diatribes, beer reviews, and clear guidelines on brewing your first batch. "So many homebrewers in Poland are

my pupils. They've learned how to homebrew from my videos."

Like America's in the early 1980s, the Polish beer scene then was largely uncharted and owed much to DIY principles. For example, resourceful homebrewers discovered that they could disconnect the rubber hose that fed water into the toilet and then remove the mesh metal cover. The hose instantly became a cost-free kettle screen to filter wort. Also as in America, the Polish homebrew movement bred the next generation of professional brewers eager to upend the status quo. Kopyra points to a pivotal moment in 2011, when Browar PINTA released the piney, resinous Atak Chmielu ("Attack of the Hops"), the first American-inspired IPA brewed in Poland. Kopyra proclaimed on his blog: "From that day, we can divide the history of Polish brewing: before Atak Chmielu and after."

FUN FACT

Poland has native hops. The most widely grown varieties are the earthy, herbal Marynka and floral, lavender-like Lublin (Lubelski).

Kopyra has the authority to make that pronouncement. He stands as one of Poland's premier beer authorities. He cofounded the Polish Homebrewers Association, wrote a

book (*Piwo*, "beer"), runs the country's biggest craft beer competition, and consults for breweries such as Widawa, where he breaks flavorful new ground. "We created the first Polish smoked porter and smoked pale ale."

Many beer scenes begin with homage, imitating that which inspires. Now Poland is formulating a brewing culture around native ingredients—not surprising given many brewers' roots. Kopyra estimates that 90 percent of the new breweries in Poland have some connection to one or more homebrewers . . . which is how fresh and smoked herrings find their way into a recipe. "It was like a foreign extra stout with a slightly strange flavor," Kopyra says of Piwoteka's Ucho Od Śledzia.

Freezing beers has become another hot trend here. Putting strong lagers in subzero conditions and removing the frozen water creates an eisbock, a boozier, more concentrated beer. Polish versions may start with a base of double IPAs, imperial stouts, and even quadrupels, such as Browar Szałpiw's Buba Extreme, aged in Cognac, calvados, or whiskey casks.

FUN FACT

Politics can drive anyone to drink, so much so that in 1990 satirist Janusz Rewiński founded the Polish Beer-Lovers' Party, its mission to promote drinking beer instead of vodka in pubs. The party won 16 parliamentary seats in 1991's election before slowly going flat.

Smoke is looming on the horizon as well. Brewers here are showing renewed interest in the indigenous grodziskie, a golden beer made with smoked wheat. Kormoran Imperium Prunum ages with smoked plums

and has become one of Poland's most desired beers—one of more than 1,500 beers to appear in Poland in 2016. "It is really a revolution," says Kopyra.

ADVICE

- "A brewer is not a pharmacist, so it doesn't matter if you use 19 grams of hops or 22 grams of hops. It's a small difference. It's not connected to sanitizing, and it's very important to have clean equipment. It's similar to Charlie Papazian's 'Relax, don't worry, have a homebrew.' It doesn't matter if your water is 63 degrees Celsius or 65 degrees. Don't worry, just brew. In Polish, it is '*Browar to nie apteka*.'"

- "One of the biggest mistakes [when using smoked malts] is to use beech-smoked malt, which gives you sausage notes. Grodziskie is made with oak-smoked malt, which is more like a fireplace."

GRODZISKIE
Smoked Polish Wheat Ale
TOMASZ KOPYRA

"Grodziskie is kind of like Polish Champagne, a highly carbonated smoked wheat beer developed in the city of Grodzisk Wielkopolski. (*Piwo Grodziskie* means "beer from Grodzisk.") It's important to use only oak-smoked wheat malt, noted for its fireplace aroma and flavor. Originally Grodzisk breweries made the beer with two yeast strains, but don't worry about complicating things. The key is to use clean ale yeast with few esters. (Avoid hefeweizen yeast and souring *Lactobacillus* bacteria.) Traditionally Grodziskie contained local Tomyski hops, a variety similar to Lubelski. You can substitute continental noble hops like Czech Saaz or German Hallertaue Mittelfrüh. Grodziskie was typically bottle-conditioned after the addition of isinglass, but if you want to serve beer from a keg, remember to reduce the amount of priming sugar."

SIZE	5 gallons (18.9 L)
ORIGINAL GRAVITY	1.031
FINAL GRAVITY	1.012
IBU	25
SRM	5
ABV	3.3%

MALTS AND ADJUNCTS
5.5 pounds (2.5 kg) Oak-Smoked Wheat Malt
1.1 pounds (0.5 kg) Rice Hulls

HOPS (90-MINUTE BOIL)
1.05 ounces (30 g) Lubelski (or Saaz) (4% AA), 90 minutes
0.7 ounce (20 g) Lubelski (or Saaz), 15 minutes

YEAST
1 package Fermentis SafAle US-05 Dry Yeast or Wyeast 1318 London Ale III

NOTES
Mash Warm up 1.3 gallons (5 L) of water to 104°F (40°C). Add malt.
Mash temperature, 98°F (37°C), 30 minutes

Add 0.5 gallon (2 L) of boiling water
Mash temperature, 122°F (50°C), 20 minutes

Add 0.8 gallon (3 L) of boiling water
Mash temperature, 158°F (70°C), 30 minutes

Mash out temperature, 169°F (76°C)

Brewing Cool wort to around 64°F (18°C).

Fermenting Ferment at 64°F (18°C) for 7 days, then use isinglass to clear the beer.

Post-fermentation Bottle with about 7 ounces (200 g) of corn sugar.

ANDY PARKER

ELUSIVE BREWING
FLEET, ENGLAND
elusivebrewing.com

Andy Parker's first sip of Sierra Nevada Pale Ale was memorable for all the wrong reasons. "I almost spit it out because it was too bitter." In the late 1990s, the Englishman was working in California's Silicon Valley and missing his English-style ales very much. So he and a friend took to his garage to homebrew a bitter—the British kind. The result was repugnant. "We went back to drinking Coors Light."

The experience stuck a fork in his brewing career for more than a decade, during which time he returned to England and developed a taste for Belgian beers. They broadened his perspective and palate, leading him to explore imports such as San Diego's Green Flash West Coast IPA. The bitterness of that hop bomb so tickled his fancy that he decided to clone it at home. No surprise there. Countless homebrewers begin by imitating a favorite beer. But he entered his clone in a competition and won bronze. Age, typically the kiss of death for an IPA, proved essential to his triumph. But consider the state of American beer exports in 2012: "The U.S. IPAs we were drinking were all three or four months old. That maybe helped me win that medal."

Until recently, Parker toiled in video streaming, working massive sporting events, including the soccer and rugby world cups. "My day job was slowly killing me. My wife could see I was breaking a little bit." Brewing

offered an outlet. In 2014, he entered his American red in a homebrew competition sponsored by the Craft Beer Co. pub chain. He won top honors: commercially brewing his recipe at Dark Star brewery and a £5,000 cash prize.

Parker kept brewing, happily taking his lumps. "I learned about every single infection you can possibly get, in one way or another, which is good grounding for being a professional brewer." He belonged to the London Amateur Brewers group, a fantastic forum for feedback, even when some beers needed work or never should've escaped a beer bottle. "There was one beer I called Aus Trappist, and it was basically a Belgian quad with lots of Australian hops. It was the most horrible thing I ever made. There was nothing technically wrong with it, in terms of brewing, but it was just an awful recipe and really bitter. I took it to the homebrew club and got some really weird looks."

FUN FACT

Cloned beers have become big business. Brooklyn Brew Shop offers kits from breweries such as Stillwater and Evil Twin, while Northern Brewer sells kits from Golden Road, Elysian, and Goose Island. AB InBev owns both the shop and breweries.

With his wife's blessing and their joint savings, Parker quit his job and started looking for a brewery location. When not pounding the pavement, he continued making beer, 20 liters at a go, every other day. "I'd brew eight batches of the same recipe trying to perfect it," he says, echoing what so many successful homebrewers say: Only by replicating beers as consistently as a photocopying machine can you become a better brewer.

FUN FACT

The London Amateur Brewers club has provided a great breeding ground for talent. Past members include Evin O'Riordain of the Kernel, Weird Beard's Bryan Spooner and Gregg Irwin, and Mick Harrison of Mix Brewery.

He found the ideal industrial digs down the road from craft upstart Siren and launched the vintage video game–inspired Elusive Brewing in 2016. Parker's five-barrel system pumps out Level Up, a red ale socked with rotating modern hops, including Citra and Rakau; Cheat Mode Stout; and Starship Fleet English Pale Ale. He happily bounces from a smoked California common to lime-squeezed witbier. "I didn't have one thing I stuck with. It turned into an obsession of wanting to brew everything."

He has discovered the key difference between kitchen and professional batches. "As a homebrewer, you can pretty much buy anything you want. If you want four ounces of Nelson Sauvin, you can buy it. If you want five kilos as a professional brewer, then join the queue."

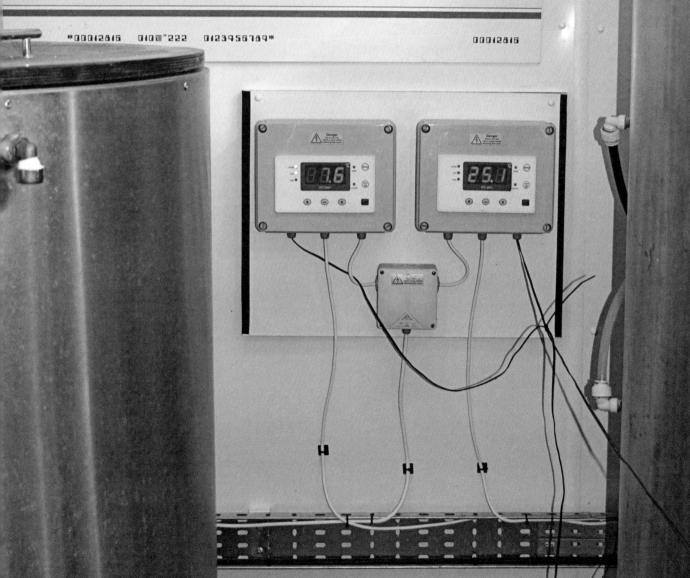

ADVICE

- "You don't have to spend lots of money to brew good beer. It's all about getting the process right, first and foremost. Keep it simple."
- "If I look at how I develop recipes now, there's probably a bit more art than science. I love to grab a bunch of different hops and rub them and figure out what will work together."

BREWER SPOTLIGHT

After a beer-and-barbecue epiphany at a Brooklyn restaurant, Logan Plant—yep, singer Robert Plant's son—bought a homebrew kit and opened Duke's Brew & Que in the Beavertown area of London. He designed beers to pair well with barbecue, such as the spicy 8 Ball Rye IPA and Smog Rocket Smoked Porter. Today, they form part of the core lineup of what has become Beavertown Brewery.

AMERICAN RED ALE
ANDY PARKER

"If you were a BJCP purist, you'd point out that American red ale is not a recognized style, but I've never really paid much attention to that. This beer won the Craft Beer Company competition. I held a large novelty check with my name on it. I was flabbergasted, completely knocked for six. Many more beers were opened and shared with friends that night, and it's one I'll never forget!"

SIZE	5.8 gallons (22.18 L)
ORIGINAL GRAVITY	1.059
FINAL GRAVITY	1.015
IBU	42
SRM	18
ABV	5.7%

MALTS AND ADJUNCTS

7.5 pounds (3.4 kg) Crisp Maris Otter

3.5 pounds (1.6 kg) Crisp Munich Malt

14 ounces (400 g) British Crystal (55°L)

6.3 ounces (180 g) British Dark Crystal

6.3 ounces (180 g) Crisp Cara Malt

4.2 ounces (120 g) Simpsons Wheat Malt

HOPS (60-MINUTE BOIL)

1.75 ounces (15 g) Simcoe (13% AA), 60 minutes

0.7 ounce (20 g) Simcoe, 15 minutes

0.7 ounce (20 g) Simcoe, 5 minutes

1.6 ounces (45 g) Simcoe, Flameout

3.5 ounces (100 g) Simcoe, Dry hop

YEAST

1 package Fermentis SafAle US-05 Dry Yeast

NOTES

Mash Mash temperature, 152°F (66°C), 60 minutes

Mash out temperature, 168°F (75°C), 15 minutes

Brewing Add 1 unit Whirlfloc with 15 minutes left in the boil.

JORGE RINGENBACH

thought I knew about beer because I used to drink Corona," says Jorge Ringenbach. "Growing up in Mexico, you think that brewing requires big Modelo facilities." His beliefs flipped after a college friend took him to Mexico City's Beer Factory, one of the country's earliest brewpubs. "Looking at the facility I thought, *I can do this*."

Ringenbach's homebrewing journey began with a pricey plunge into the unknown. Inspired by Sam Calagione's story of starting Dogfish Head with a half-barrel Sabco Brew-Magic—which today starts at $7,000—Ringenbach ordered a similar system, a foolhardy yet optimistic move. "I bought it without any notion of how to brew." The other issue? Ingredients, specifically the lack thereof.

Ringenbach road-tripped to Austin and San Antonio to stock up on enough hops and malt to last a year. He brewed in his basement, listening to brewing podcasts such as *Brewing with Style*. "I would apply everything I heard in the podcasts to my beers and taste it. That way, every time I brewed I was able to correct some part of the brewing process. It was a lot of practice."

It paid off in 2011 when his Sierra Nevada Pale Ale replica took best of show at the Copa Cerveza México competition (page 56). "It was a combination of luck and there weren't a lot of homebrewers." Ringenbach

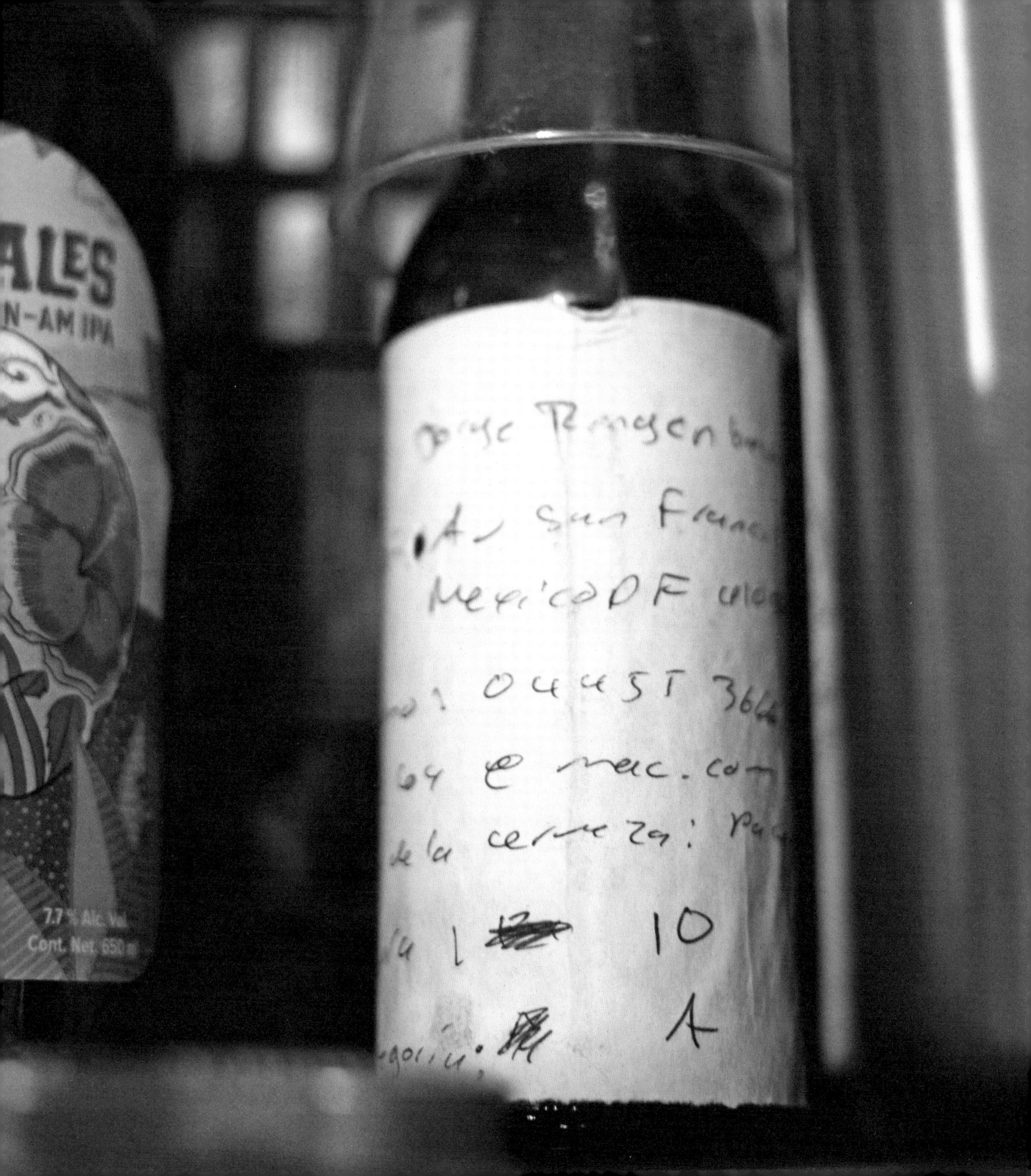
ALES
N-AM IPA
7.7 % Alc. Vol.
Mexico DF
@ mac.com
cerveza
10
A

laughs. "One of the best ways to test your skills is with an audience, and I always wanted other people to try my beer." He bought a kegerator and placed it in his friends' restaurant with simple instructions: Drink every drop and return the kegs so he could brew another batch.

The restaurateurs adored Ringenbach's porter so much that they were willing to break their exclusivity contract with Grupo Modelo—a common tactic in Mexico, where megabreweries dole out free beer, TVs, and furniture and even finance bar renovations—to put his beer permanently on tap. At that, the lawyer turned his amateur pursuit into Cervecería Escollo, a moniker that requires explanation.

Fun Fact

A federal ruling in 2013 limited such sugarcoated arrangements, which leveled the playing field for beer produced locally.

Ringenbach felt his German last name lacked the right ring for a Mexican beer brand, though. "Escollo is the name of the street where I live, so that's as local as I could get." He also liked the word's meaning: obstacle. His up-and-coming brewery overcomes the obstacle of Mexico's lime-spritzed status quo with pilsners, porters, double IPAs, pale ales, and sours. "With brewing, one of the most important things for me is diversity."

He hasn't quit his day job yet, however. "I'm still a lawyer. It's easier to make money out of the law than out of brewing." But Ringenbach isn't mothballing his basement brewing equipment any time soon, either.

"I just homebrewed two weeks ago. I will always be a homebrewer at heart."

ADVICE

- "Start doing it and lose the fear of brewing. Whether it's 1 gallon or 15 barrels, the spirit of brewing is the same. Only the dimensions change."
- "You need to be the worst judge of your beer. If not, you will get stuck in mediocrity."

BREWER SPOTLIGHT

Jamil Zainasheff, cohost of *Brewing with Style* (thebrewingnetwork.com), went from homebrew savant who wrote *Brewing Classic Styles* and *Yeast* to founder of Heretic Brewing Company in Fairfield, California. Drink his dank Evil Cousin Imperial IPA.

ESCOLLO PORTER
JORGE RINGENBACH

"This porter helped me make the transition from homebrewer to professional brewer. At the time, almost all the beer consumed in Mexico City was light lager, and this was a disruption in color and flavor. I enjoy this beer with many Mexican dishes, and it remains one of our top sellers."

SIZE	5 gallons (18.9 L)
ORIGINAL GRAVITY	1.062
FINAL GRAVITY	1.016
IBU	35
SRM	26
ABV	5.8%

MALTS AND ADJUNCTS

7.3 pounds (3.3 kg) German Pale Ale Malt (2.3°L)

2.1 pounds (0.95 kg) German Munich Malt (10°L)

7 ounces (200 g) American Crystal Malt 40 (40°L)

7 ounces (200 g) American Crystal Malt 60 (60°L)

7 ounces (200 g) American Chocolate Malt (350°L)

7 ounces (200 g) Flaked Barley (2.2°L)

2.3 ounces (65 g) American Blackprinz Malt (500°L)

HOPS (60-MINUTE BOIL)

0.5 ounce (14 g) Magnum (13% AA), 60 minutes

0.2 ounce (5 g) East Kent Golding (4.7% AA), 15 minutes

YEAST

1 package Fermentis SafAle US-05 Dry Yeast

NOTES

Mash Mash temperature, 151°F (66°C), 60 minutes

Mash out temperature, 158°F (70°C), 15 minutes

Brewing Add 0.5 teaspoon (2.2 g) yeast nutrient with 15 minutes left in the boil. Cool wort to around 70°F (21°C).

Fermenting Ferment at 65°F (20°C) for 7–10 days.

Post-fermentation Cold crash at 32°F (0°C) for 1 week.

COPA CERVEZA MEXICO

MEXICO CITY
copacerveza.mx

In Mexico, mass-produced lagers Corona and Tecate reign supreme, served cold and crowned with limes—or at least that's how it looks north of the border. Truth is, Mexico is cultivating a homegrown beer culture that's growing rapidly although still playing catch-up to America. "I think we're 20 years behind," says José Ruíz, but his efforts are closing the gap.

He lived near Detroit from 2004 to 2008, picking up homebrewing as a hobby that proved nearly impossible to continue in Chihuahua City. "I didn't find any homebrew stores. I saw the need for myself as well as the opportunity to sell ingredients to everybody." He filled the void by founding brewing-supply importer and distributor Maltas e Insumos Cerveceros, followed by the Copa Cerveza Mexico brewing competition. (It started in Guadalajara in 2009 and now occurs annually in Mexico City.)

Copa Cerveza first featured professional beers, but Ruíz turned the 2011 edition over to homebrewers. Accredited members of the nonprofit Beer Judge Certification Program, the international gold standard for accreditation, rated and reviewed the one hundred entries. "It was a new experience for all the homebrewers," says Ruíz. Judges

assessed beers live to help brewers better understand the evaluation process, separating the flawed from the fantastic.

In-person education is essential in Mexico. There's scant beer-making literature in Spanish, and YouTube videos often serve as a primary instructional resource. Nonetheless, the country's collective level of brewing education is increasing, partly due to Copa Cerveza. It's now Mexico's largest beer competition, running parallel contests for amateur and professional brewers. "We've created the interest for people to become beer judges. Now there are more than 50 Mexican BJCP judges. With more knowledge, people are making better beer."

Mexico now has nearly a dozen homebrew shops, and Ruíz sees more homebrewers joining the pro ranks, despite the amount of capital required for commercial equipment, fighting the conglomerates' lime-squeezed grip, and small demand. As in America, a country needs only a couple of decades to reshape its brewing landscape, and craft and independent beer in the States possesses a solid double-digit market share. "Right now the target is one percent," says Ruíz. "But I think we can double that."

KEVIN RYAN

○

JOHANNESBURG, SOUTH AFRICA

ronically, Kevin Ryan never caught the brewing bug while working as an electrical engineer for South African Breweries back in the 1980s. Beer was work, plain and simple, and he never dreamed of taking his job home.

Fast forward a few decades. Ryan attended a summer celebration put on by Wort Hog Brewers, the country's largest homebrew club. Although he was a member, he never brewed, a quirk quashed after a homebrewer he met at the festival invited him over for a brew day. "I went to this guy's house and saw how easy it was: He was brewing a barley wine and had it quite under control," Ryan said. "I thought, *I can do this.* I've been brewing ever since."

He came to brewing late, but Ryan made up for lost time. He filled his *pondok*—a Malaysian word for a little shack—with kettles and kegs and toted them to his carport to brew English ESBs and brown ales while aging Belgian dark strong ales in wooden barrels. He became chairman of Wort Hog Brewers, an organization so homespun and handcrafted that it commissioned a plastics firm to produce custom brewing equipment. Ryan started with that plastic setup before graduating to the Grainfather electric system.

"Ten or eleven years ago, there were no homebrew shops. There was no source of ingredients." Homebrewers visited Drayman's brewery, where Wort Hog founder Moritz Kallmeyer supplied them with healthy yeast. South African Breweries (now part of AB InBev) sold them hops and malt—black or pale—for a song. "They have to sell malt and hops to the public at the same price they sell to themselves," Ryan revealed. "It works out to be half or a quarter of the price of buying imported hops." Homebrew shops dot the nation today, a drastic change in just a decade.

Fun Fact

The Brewers Co-op in Cape Town consists of an evolving collective of 16 amateur brewers—accountants, dentists, and even DJs—who share the same set of equipment and brew everything from Bohemian pilsners to rooibos-infused blonde ales. Visit them at Brewers.coop.

In addition to using homegrown hops (page 61), local brewers set themselves apart by incorporating indigenous teas, including earthy, vanilla-like rooibos and herbs such as African wormwood and pungent buchu. "People often put it in brandy as a restorative when they're feeling sick," Ryan explained. Other brewers have tried to refine *umqombothi*, a traditional African brew made with corn and sorghum, fermented spontaneously, and thick and tangy as yogurt. "Many people treat it like food because it's really like a porridge. It's still actively fermenting when you buy it."

Ryan organized South Africa's annual national homebrew competition, giving him a firsthand taste of the country's rising amateur beer scene. "It's a breeding ground for craft brewers," who still face obstacles on the

road to going pro. "We have a very complicated licensing system here. It could take a year to get a brewing license, and in the meantime you need to have the premises because they'll need to come inspect it. You can't start selling a beer until you get a license. It's quite a big deterrent."

ADVICE

Be resourceful. "One thing that we South African homebrewers don't get so easily is liquid yeast. Because people can't just go to the store and buy yeast, there's a culture of people keeping their own yeast libraries and cultures."

IN MEMORIAM

Kevin Ryan died unexpectedly in May 2017 during production of this book.

SOUTH AFRICAN HOPS

The uniquely aromatic, fragrant hop varieties developed by farmers and researchers worldwide make today's memorable IPAs possible. Germany's hits include the citrusy Mandarina Bavaria. The Pacific Northwest contributed tropical Citra and berrylike Mosaic. Australia and New Zealand offer melonesque Galaxy and white wine–like Nelson Sauvin, respectively.

The new frontier for hops lies in South Africa, however, where breeders have developed a swell of singular varieties. Southern Passion merges the spicy grassiness of European noble hops with berries

and passion fruit. Southern Aroma has a pointedly floral, herbal bent, while African Queen—released in May 2015 after 12 years of research—flaunts a tropical, citrusy complexity with echoes of blackcurrants and chiles as well as a sturdy bitterness. Breweries such as Cellarmaker, La Cumbre, Modern Times, and Firestone Walker have embraced South African varieties, though they may have a tougher time acquiring them in the future. In 2017, AB InBev—which acquired SABMiller, the owner of the SAB Hop Farms—decided to keep the entire harvest of proprietary hops for themselves.

SATURDAY SESSION SAISON
KEVIN RYAN

This saison was one of the last beers that Kevin ever brewed. Sadly, he never had a chance to taste the finished beer. The Wort Hop Brewers Summer Beer Festival served it to toast to Kevin's life.

SIZE	5 gallons (18.9 L)
ORIGINAL GRAVITY	1.58
FINAL GRAVITY	1.12
IBU	32
SRM	7
ABV	6%

MALTS AND ADJUNCTS
6.6 pounds (3 kg) SAB Pale Malt
4.4 pounds (2 kg) Best Malz Red X
1.1 pounds (500 g) Rolled Oats

HOPS (60-MINUTE BOIL)
2.82 ounces (80 g) Southern Passion (10% AA), 10 minutes
2 ounces (50 g) Southern Aroma (5% AA), Flameout

YEAST
1 packet Mangrove Jack's M29 French Saison

NOTES
Water Profile (additions to the original water)
0.282 ounce (8.02 g) calcium chloride (⅔ in mashwater, ⅓ in sparge)
0.085 ounce (2.42 g) calcium sulphate (⅔ in mashwater, ⅓ in sparge)
0.01 ounce (0.3 g) salt (⅔ in mashwater, ⅓ in sparge)

Mash Protein Rest (optional), 129°F (54°C), 30 minutes
Mash temperature, 148°F (64°C), 60-75 minutes
Mash out temperature, 167°F (75°C), 10-15 minutes
Sparge, 167°F (75°C)

Fermenting Ferment at 82°F (28°C) until reaching final gravity.

CALEB SELBY

SUZHOU, CHINA

This Indiana native had brewed 17 or 18 batches of imperial IPAs with his brother-in-law. They'd even dabbled in barley wines and boozy stouts. Selby naturally fantasized about starting a brewery. After all, how hard could it be? The two men raised funds just as the Midwest market yawned wide in the early 2010s.

But the best-laid plans often go awry. Selby's wife, Darcy, accepted a job in China. In summer 2013, the family packed up their belongings and made the intercontinental leap to Suzhou, near Shanghai. They and their three children spent the next five years living in the Suzhou Industrial Park, a joint partnership between Singapore and China developed to attract Western companies. The Selbys joined a 100,000-strong expat community, many of them thirsting for a well-made pint.

In Selby's words: "The first thing almost every expat I met said was, 'You need to start making beer over here. The beer is crap.'" Mass-produced lagers, including Tsingtao and Snow, had flooded the Chinese market, plus Belgian imports such as Chimay and Westmalle. "That's what we were surviving on when we first got over here."

Selby never intended to work a nine-to-five in China. The former HR specialist wanted to keep the home fires burning, "but I didn't want to stagnate. That's why I took on real serious brewing. I thought, *Let me tackle this as a research project where I can get as much intellectually developed while I have the freedom and opportunity to do that, then be prepared to come back and have my feet underneath me.*"

He launched Zanolious Brewing in his garage, outfitted with convenience store–style refrigerators and a 20-gallon brew system. (The name is made up; he wanted a *Z* for a logo.) Glass carboys proved prohibitively expensive, so he built his fermentation system around dirt-cheap five-gallon stainless steel kegs. "I figured out I could ferment in corny kegs," he says of the vessels traditionally used by the soda industry to dispense drinks.

FUN FACT

Snow, a lager sold mainly in China, is the world's best-selling beer.

His brewing repertoire encompasses a California common, Oktoberfest-ready Märzen, kölsch, and an imperial lager hit with New Zealand hops. An average month features two or three 20-gallon batches. He bottles most of his production, selling beer to expats clandestinely via social media and distributing kegs to a local bar where he has a dedicated line. He doesn't have a government license, but that's a bit of a gray area in Suzhou—and much of China—where street vendors often sling noodles and lamb skewers without permits. "It's the Wild West over here. It's a developing country to some extent, and this is not on the radar yet."

Homebrewing in China has its challenges, though, most prominently the language barrier. "I had some

welding done for me basically through charades and sharing an iPhone," says Selby, who is taking Mandarin lessons. He brought brewing parts from America, including a plate chiller and carbon dioxide regulators and gauges . . . only to discover that China threads its equipment differently. "I'd have four different fittings to get from the American thread to what I needed to attach to the Chinese part."

Sourcing ingredients also poses a struggle in Suzhou, where the local homebrew shop leaves open bags of hops sitting on room-temperature shelves. Word of mouth led Selby to a Shanghai local who imports hops, grains, and yeasts and then sells them from his house. That convenience comes with a 200 to 250 percent markup. Selby mitigates his costs by buying Chinese grains and smuggling. "I probably have homebrew ingredients shipped to a couple dozen different addresses in the U.S., and people that are back for business just fill up a suitcase and bring it back to me."

The family plans to return to Indiana after Darcy's contract expires in 2018. There, Selby wants to open a fully licensed brick-and-mortar Zanolious. Until then, he keeps brewing in his garage, inviting neighbors for tastes from his taps and unfiltered criticism. "I'm in an expat community that capably represents the world." Czechs critique his pilsners, Belgians weigh in on his Westvleteren clone, and Germans assess his Märzen. "The Germans, they are not restrained in their feedback," he says, laughing.

Each critique helps Selby fine-tune his skillset, putting him closer to a professional career years in the making. "If we were going to start a brewery back in 2011, when I had made something like 17 batches of imperial IPA . . . I was woefully underprepared."

ADVICE

"Bell's Hopslam really turned me on. That's a sit-down experience, especially if you're a novice and are attracted to hoppy beers. We had that and thought, *This is, like, $19 a six-pack. If we make a 50-bottle batch and get it right, we can save lots of money and be proud of ourselves.* We were chasing the Hopslam dream. You can get anybody interested in drinking big imperial IPAs, but it's not a training-wheels beer. You need to cut your teeth on something more petite and graduate people into that style."

FAR (FROM AN) EASTERN THING
Hoppy Lager
CALEB SELBY

"This imaginative lager pays homage to the stunning raw ingredients originating from New Zealand. Although made in China (like all the best stuff), New Zealand ingredients make this beer what it is. Look for solid New Zealand malts and the freshest Motueka hops you can find, especially for dry hopping."

SIZE	5 gallons (18.9 L)
ORIGINAL GRAVITY	1.074
FINAL GRAVITY	1.015
IBU	32
SRM	10
ABV	7.75%

MALTS AND ADJUNCTS

14 pounds (6.3 kg) New Zealand 2-Row Pilsner Malt

0.2 pound (90 g) Crystal Malt 20°L

0.45 pound (204 g) Biscuit Malt

HOPS (60-MINUTE BOIL)

0.5 ounce (14 g) Motueka (8.2% AA), First wort hop

0.5 ounce (14 g) Motueka, 45 minutes

1–2 ounces (28–56 g) Motueka, Dry hop

YEAST

2 packages Fermentis SafLager 34/70 Dry Yeast

NOTES

Mash Multistep mash: 105°F (40°C), 20 minutes

133°F (56°C), 10 minutes

152°F (70°C), 60 minutes

158°F (70°C), 10 minutes

Mash out temperature, 168°F (75°C), 15 minutes

Adjust sparge water pH to 5.3.

Fermenting Aerate wort prior to yeast pitch. Pitch yeast above 65°F (18°C), then slowly cool to 54°F (12°C) over the first 24 hours. Ferment at 54°F (12°C) until terminal gravity is reached (do not rack to secondary).

Post-fermentation Once terminal gravity is reached, rack to keg along with 1–2 ounces (28–56 g) of Motueka whole-cone hops and allow for 2–4 weeks of diacetyl rest at above 68°F (20°C). Transfer keg to cold storage for lagering. Lager for at least 3–4 weeks before serving. Based on personal preference, hops can be left in the keg or removed once carbonation begins.

MATTHIAS STEINBERG

One day, six or seven years ago, Matthias Steinberg—mechanical engineering hobbyist and CFO for a tech company that counts GoDaddy as a competitor—had an idea: Why not make beer? He ordered a kit from eBay with precrushed grains, and then he crushed his first batch. Brewing proved both intoxicating and inspirational. "I suddenly realized it would be an amazing project to build a brewing rig. I could combine two things that I really liked doing."

He banged on his Berlin balcony for days on end, welding and assembling pipes, tweaking and testing. His neighbors watched, puzzled, wondering what he was constructing. One cold December day, he fired up his creation. Clouds of vapor rose into the sky.

"Somebody came to me on the balcony and said, 'Everybody is wondering what you are doing.'" He was brewing beer. Steinberg might as well have said he was simmering stray cats. "Germans are still conditioned to believe that some industrial, middle-of-the-road pilsner is as good as it gets. For many people, it's a huge surprise that it can be done on a DIY system."

But the first test drive of the Beast ended in disaster. Steinberg and his friend Rory Lawton were brewing a massive imperial stout loaded with oats and smoked malt. The brew day was coming to a close when a pump jammed. Some 20 liters of steamy, inky wort coursed onto the kitchen floor. "We'd spent five or six hours brewing, and I screwed it up. Then we spent three hours cleaning the kitchen. Ever since, I've been working on improving a brewing rig."

To be fair, it's not any old rig. Steinberg has spent more than five years calibrating the Beast, a modular setup outfitted with several 40-liter stainless steel vessels, two electric heaters, pumps recirculating water at precise computer-controlled temperatures, and sensors feeding data to an iPhone app so Steinberg can monitor fluctuations and pH from his couch. "My goal is to build a machine that makes it less of a hassle and faster to brew."

Homebrewers often receive praise for far-out recipes that toss coffee into cream ales and use yeast strains harvested from felled trees. Steinberg has zero interest in writing outré recipes. Instead, he embodies the German pursuit of technical engineering, perfecting the mechanics and simplifying the process. He wants each batch to be unwavering and endlessly replicable.

Steinberg regularly dismantles and rebuilds the Beast, each version requiring him to relearn the system. He brews the same recipes over and over again to ensure the Beast is getting better. He doesn't want to make a million euros from his masterpiece; rather, he sees the Beast as his gift to the global homebrew community. "The Beast can grow with your ambition," he says of the

modular setup, which can easily be scaled up or down. Steinberg plans to post the system's specs online for free. "It's like an open-source hardware project. I want people to be able to start building their own and keep improving it."

ADVICE

"I was surprised how easy it was to produce something very drinkable. But that comes with a caveat: In the beginning, you want to stick with an easy, good recipe and try to nail that. The real challenge is when people believe they can quickly put together their own recipes."

KITCHEN FLOOR IMPERIAL STOUT
RORY LAWTON & MATTHIAS STEINBERG

Developed by Steinberg's brewing partner, Rory Lawton, Kitchen Floor takes its name from their brewing disaster in which nearly an entire batch spewed onto the kitchen floor. But not all was lost. "After the accident, we salvaged one liter of the brew, which turned out to be excellent!" says Steinberg.

SIZE	5 gallons (18.9 L)
ORIGINAL GRAVITY	1.074
FINAL GRAVITY	1.010
IBU	77
SRM	58
ABV	8.5%

MALTS AND ADJUNCTS

9.9 pounds (4.5 kg) German Pilsner

4.4 pounds (2 kg) Flaked Oats

1.1 pounds (0.5 kg) CaraMunich Malt (35°L)

1.1 pounds (0.5 kg) Chocolate Malt (350°L)

1.1 pounds (0.5 kg) Chocolate Malt (200°L)

1.1 pounds (0.5 kg) Roasted Barley (250°L)

1.1 pounds (0.5 kg) Weyermann Beech Smoked Barley Malt

HOPS (60-MINUTE BOIL)

2.6 ounces (75 g) Cascade (5.7% AA), 60 minutes

2.6 ounces (75 g) Centennial (10% AA), 60 minutes

2.6 ounces (75 g) Cascade, 15 minutes

2.6 ounces (75 g) Centennial, 5 minutes

YEAST

2 packages Wyeast 1056 American Ale

NOTES

Mash Mash temperature, 156°F (69°C), 45 minutes

Sparge temperature, 169°F (76°C)

Fermenting Ferment at 70°F (21°C).

Post-fermentation Bottle with 6 tablespoons (93.5 g) table sugar for 2.3 volumes CO_2. Store at 64°F (18°C) for 30 days.

FEDERICO ZANETTI

SANTINA CERVEZA ARTESANAL
BUENOS AIRES, ARGENTINA
facebook.com/santinacervezaartesanal

Beer can flourish far from its native lands. Cases in point: Belgian tripels in Taiwan, British stouts in Spain, and American amber in Federico Zanetti's garage in Argentina. In 2016, judges at the prestigious Somos Cerveceros competition named Zanetti the country's top homebrewer, rewarding his obsession. "I'll brew the same style four to five times before a competition, then I choose the best for the competition." He specializes in the classics—Scottish ales, porters, rauchbiers, and Belgian blondes—and you can find all of them at Santina Cerveza Artesanal, the brewery he launched in 2017.

He favors the American amber ale, though, proudly malt-forward and not mauled by hops. Try it as a counterpoint to Andy Parker's recipe (page 44). "Malty beers were my first love," says Zanetti.

FUN FACT

Martín Boan and his wife, Carolina Pérez, run the Center of Cata de Cervezas in Buenos Aires. Their beer programs and classes have trained a generation of Argentinean brewers, both amateur and professional. Boan also founded BA Malt SA, which manufactures specialty grains for brewers.

ADVICE

"When you're buying ingredients, always look for quality, and don't think about the cost. The quality of your ingredients can be the difference between a good beer and a great beer. Also, don't be afraid to blend yeast strains to create more complexity. We don't always have access to liquid yeast in Argentina, so sometimes we have to get creative."

BREWER SPOTLIGHT

Zanetti isn't the only homebrewer to fall for amber ales. Chris Trogner, who later founded Tröegs Independent Brewing with his brother John, brewed Fletcher's Better Bitter, named after his dog Fletch. "It was the basis for Hopback Amber Ale, and the recipe has hardly changed," says John.

AMBER ALE
FEDERICO ZANETTI

"This beer showcases the complexity of malts, but it is also very resinous, piney, and a little fruity. My goal is to find balance and drinkability while also showing off the hops."

SIZE	5 gallons (18.9 L)
ORIGINAL GRAVITY	1.050
FINAL GRAVITY	1.012
IBU	28
SRM	13
ABV	5%

MALTS AND ADJUNCTS
8.1 pounds (3.7 kg) Pilsner Malt
9 ounces (250 g) Caramel Malt (60°L)
8 ounces (225 g) Weyermann CaraAroma Malt
5.25 ounces (150 g) Briess Carapils
0.9 ounce (25 g) Castle Château Chocolat Malt

HOPS (60-MINUTE BOIL)
0.1 ounce (2 g) Columbus (15% AA), First wort hop
0.5 ounce (15 g) Simcoe (13% AA), 15 minutes
0.5 ounce (15 g) Amarillo (9% AA), 15 minutes
0.7 ounce (20 g) Simcoe, 5 minutes
0.7 ounce (20 g) Columbus, Flameout
0.7 ounce (20 g) Simcoe, Flameout
0.7 ounce (20 g) Amarillo, Flameout
0.9 ounce (25 g) Columbus, Dry hop 5 days
0.9 ounce (25 g) Simcoe, Dry hop 5 days
0.9 ounce (25 g) Amarillo, Dry hop 5 days

YEAST
1 package Fermentis SafAle US-05 Dry Yeast

NOTES
Mash Mash temperature, 153°F (67°C), 60 minutes
Mash all malts except chocolate malt. Add chocolate malt during the *vorlauf,* or recirculation.

Brewing Add 0.5 teaspoon (2 g) Irish moss with 15 minutes left in the boil. Add 1 pinch (0.3 g) yeast nutrient with 10 minutes left in the boil.

Fermenting Ferment at 64°F (18°C) for 5 days.

Post-fermentation Cold crash at 35°F (2°C) for 2 weeks after dry hopping.

MARK ZAPPASODI

BREWERY SILVATICUS
AMESBURY, MASSACHUSETTS
silvaticusbeers.com

The undead arrived too late to save Mark Zappasodi's music career. The New York City bassist had picked away the better part of a decade in the Serpentines, a horror-themed band playing songs about zombies, werewolves, and other dark creatures, but the rigors of touring had exacted their toll by the time he had hit his midthirties. "When your wife starts going on vacation without you and your kids are growing up and you don't see them, it starts to eat at you," he says. "I was 34, and it's pitiful for rock stars to get older. I gracefully bowed out."

But as one creative outlet faded, another arose. Zappasodi had long been a beer guy, rhapsodizing about rustic Belgians, so his wife bought him a beer kit. "She was like, 'You've been talking about it forever. You might as well just do it.' "

The musician and union painter started brewing in his small Brooklyn apartment and then in a larger Staten Island spread, where he raised hops. "With homebrewing, there are only two avenues: You do it once and you're compelled to do it all the time, or you go, 'That was fun, but I can go buy a six-pack.' I became obsessed, and it became my new art form. I was doing art, five gallons at a time."

These days, Zappasodi's hitting all the right notes with Brewery Silvaticus (Latin for "sylvan," "woodsy," or "wild"), which was born in the heavily forested Tamarack

Farmstead of rural Merrimac, Massachusetts. Here he has spent the last five years refining his approach to smoked beers, spruced ales, and old-world saisons on Brewing as Art, a steampunk-inspired steel device. The contraption—a collaboration with metal sculptor Scott van Campen—welds together form and function. "The idea was to make people stop and think, *Well, brewing is an art, too.* It was basically a custom homebrew sculpture, and it gave me the opportunity to brew like crazy. I brewed constantly, multiple times a week for many years. Do that and you'll learn the process so well."

Zappasodi originally wanted to open a Staten Island brewpub, but that plan died after the opportunity arose to buy his wife's family farmstead and they determined, "A farm brewery is the Holy Grail. We might as well chuck it all and start from scratch and build a brewery from the ground-up." He didn't want the monstrous weight of a bank loan, though, so he partnered with buddy and lager-loving brewer Jay Bullen, formerly of Alaska's 49th State Brewing, to bring Silvaticus to life. That meant planting hops and fine-tuning recipes and taste buds. "I can pick up on all the nuances and pick out a flaw from a mile away," says Zappasodi, citing his five-year odyssey. "My palate is that much better, and my brewing is that much better. That's why it was great for me not to be in the pro beer world."

Silvaticus opened in an old mill building in nearby Amesbury in summer 2017 with classic German lagers served alongside saisons hopped with farm-harvested flowers, but Zappasodi formally retired Brewing as Art, displaying it as a museum piece at the brewery. "It's done its job and brewed its last batch of beer." Though the national market is increasingly crowded, he sees fertile ground locally. "My timing for brewing was really good."

ADVICE

"Brewing a ton and drinking beers to sharpen your palate are the two most important things you can do as a brewer. If you're ambitious, you'll learn all the ones and zeroes."

BREWER SPOTLIGHT

If you like locally grown hops and grains, try the tart Field Beer by Derek Dellinger, head brewer at Kent Falls, Connecticut's first farmhouse brewery, and author of *The Fermented Man*, which chronicles his yearlong journey to eat only fermented foods.

BELGIAN TRIPEL
MARK ZAPPASODI

"This beer is pretty balanced out of the gate but will improve with age on tap. There is a saying in the homebrew world that the last few glasses of the keg are always the best. Store the bottles at room temperature, and you should be ready to start sampling in about two weeks. This beer will age spectacularly if stored in the right conditions. I've had tripels like this age in my cellar for close to a decade."

SIZE	5 gallons (18.9 L)
ORIGINAL GRAVITY	1.088
FINAL GRAVITY	1.016
IBU	50
SRM	5
ABV	9.4%

MALTS AND ADJUNCTS

14 pounds (6.35 kg) Franco/Belgian Pilsner Malt

1 pound (0.45 kg) Light Belgian Candi Sugar

HOPS (90-MINUTE BOIL)

1 ounce (28 g) Hallertau (5% AA), 60 minutes

1 ounce (28 g) Saaz (4.6% AA), 15 minutes

1 ounce (28 g) Hallertau/Saaz Blend 50/50, 5 minutes

YEAST

2 packages (2 L Starter) Wyeast 3787 Trappist Style High Gravity

NOTES

Mash Acid Rest (optional), 100°F (38°C), 120 minutes

Mash temperature, 151°F (66°C), 60 minutes

Mash out temperature (optional), 170°F (77°C), 15 minutes

Sparge temperature, 175°F (79°C)

Collect 7 gallons of wort.

Brewing Add candi sugar at flameout. Add 1 Whirlfloc tablet with 15 minutes left in the boil. Cool wort to around 60°F (16°C). Aerate with pure oxygen for 60 seconds.

Fermenting Ferment at 60–62°F (16–17°C) for 2 weeks. At terminal gravity, rack into secondary for 7–10 days.

Post-fermentation

Keg carbonate at 10–15PSI for 7–10 days or bottle condition with 1 cup (340 g) dextrose. Allow to age for a minimum of 2 weeks up to several years.

J. B. ZORN

CHARLESTON, SOUTH CAROLINA

Hailing from a family of mariners, J. B. Zorn enrolled in the U.S. Merchant Marine Academy in Kings Point, New York, soon learning the ins and outs of the life aquatic—beer included.

One long weekend on leave, he and his dad cracked into a homebrew kit and brewed the kind of lager you make without regard to sanitation or temperature control. "It was pretty rough," Zorn says, laughing. Rather than leaving their newfound hobby bobbing dead in the water, father and son kept at it. "We had a couple regimental officers who were super-supportive." When he turned 21, his superiors began sharing British beers with the freshly legal midshipman, who brewed IPAs such as Commodore Hopenfield.

Post-graduation, Zorn joined the Coast Guard, and his first tour of duty took him to Honolulu. While it was paradise on the one hand, on the other hand, blah beer. Selection was limited, and long transit times dulled flavors. "Everybody has a craft beer journey, especially homebrewers. As you start to brew, you try to make things you can't buy at the store." And when you're in the Coast Guard, you forever hanker for a taste of a previous home.

Over the last decade, Zorn has sailed from Honolulu to Monterey, California; then Fairfax, Virginia; and now he is based in Charleston. He totes his brewing stand—welded by a fellow coastie in Hawaii—across the country, constantly acquiring new equipment and skills. The certified cicerone trained as a systems engineer

but spends his days as a marine investigator. The methodologies for both jobs fit his homebrewing hobby as snugly as a wet suit. "What factors might've led to why this beer didn't turn out? Was it the recipe? Was it the ingredients? Was it the yeast?" Constantly relocating also provides its own set of challenges to solve on the brewing side. "Everywhere I go, I've got to completely readdress how I'm going to do water, how I'm going to do cooling, and all these things."

In Hawaii, he brewed a saison on New Year's Eve and went to a party where he met a woman named Rachel an hour before midnight. A year or so later, he brewed her another saison—her favorite style—bottled it, and labeled it with a marriage proposal. Their wedding featured handmade beers: Pop's Hops Imperial IPA for his dad, Big Ron's Maple Brown Ale for his father-in-law, and, in lieu of a mother-son dance, a mother-son homebrew toast.

In Monterey, he brewed rye IPAs and saisons in his garage. In Virginia, he and his dad built a shed in the backyard, brewing outside before transferring wort to the basement for temperature-stable fermentation. "It was a little bit farmhousey." In Charleston, the biggest challenge was installing a water line in the garage that also features a TV, a chest freezer, a 10-gallon brewing system, and three taps offering his preferred pale ales and dry West Coast IPAs, as well as stylistic stalwarts such as dubbels and stouts. "For me, weird and unique is not the ultimate goal. I'd rather put my stamp on a classic pilsner or pale ale and make it at home and make it fresh."

Zorn has two kids of his own now, so, like many Costco-convert parents, he prefers to buy in bulk. He stocks his garage with 50-pound sacks of grain and his freezer with plenty of hop pellets. "At any one time, I can brew pretty much any style based on what I have on hand. I keep three or four different kinds of yeast and a couple hundred pounds of grain, just in case." He's as keen to test new recipes as he is to revise past efforts. Nothing ever stays static for Zorn, but that's the life he signed up for. "Moving every couple of years isn't for everybody, but at the same time it's not this opportunity that everybody has."

ADVICE

- "You can brew great beer with one pot. You don't need a three-vessel system with pumps and a wort chiller. You can do it with minimal equipment."

- "Keep on learning, keep on talking to people, and don't be afraid when you fail. You can make it better. I've made some beer multiple times, back to back, because I'm like, *This is all off. I'm going to redo it.* You're going to get to a point where you're making consistently good beer. When you start, you might be making good or great beer three or four times out of ten. Hopefully as you keep brewing, you're making good or great beer eight to nine times out of ten. For a hobby, that's a pretty good ratio."

- If your batch goes awry, look to your yeast strain, and don't reuse it too many times. "Get some fresh yeast, and that beer will be a home run each time."

- "Brewing with people is always going to be more informative than with a particular book. One style of brewing is not going to work for everybody. Measuring the pH each time and doing a triple decoction isn't necessary for each beer. You can make great single-infusion pale ales by using fresh ingredients, making your starter, using the right yeast, and using enough of it."

BREWER SPOTLIGHT

If, like Zorn's wife, Rachel, you like saisons, check out Mike Karnowski. He owned a New Orleans homebrew shop and wrote *Homebrew Beyond the Basics* before opening Zebulon Artisan Ales near Asheville, North Carolina. He concentrates on bottle-conditioned farmhouse and historic ales as well as sour and wild ales, rarely repeating any of them.

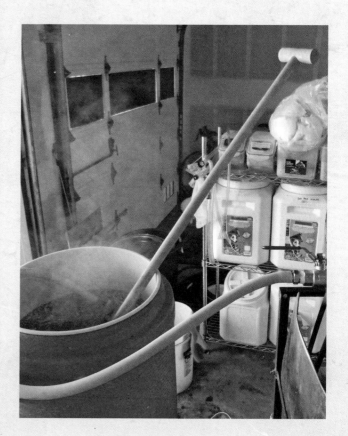

SERENDIPITY SAISON
J. B. ZORN

"At its best, the saison style is eminently approachable and individual to each brewer. This recipe is fairly simple but encompasses the spirit of a traditional saison at a higher ABV, highlighting elements of yeast-derived lemon, pepper, and fruit esters married with fragrant noble hops that provide a harmonious herbal-floral quality. 'Serendipity' is a fitting name, as this was one of my first original homebrew recipes that I brewed the day I met my wife, Rachel. Naturally, I brewed a new batch for my wedding proposal a year later."

SIZE	5 gallons (18.9 L)
ORIGINAL GRAVITY	1.072
FINAL GRAVITY	1.015
IBU	24
SRM	1
ABV	7.9%

MALTS AND ADJUNCTS

9 pounds (4.1 kg) German Pilsner Malt

1.25 pounds (566 g) German Vienna Malt

8 ounces (226 g) Wheat Malt

1 pound (450 g) Demerara/Cane Sugar

HOPS (90-MINUTE BOIL)

1 ounce (28 g) Styrian Golding (4.5% AA), 75 minutes

0.75 ounce (21 g) Styrian Golding, 20 minutes

1 ounce (28 g) German Spalt (2.3% AA), 10 minutes

YEAST

2 packages (2 L Starter) White Labs WLP568 Belgian Style Saison Ale Yeast Blend

NOTES

Mash Mash temperature, 148°F (64°C), 45 minutes

Mash step temperature, 154°F (68°C), 44 minutes

Brewing Add Demerara sugar and 0.5 teaspoon each (2.2 g) of yeast nutrient and Irish moss with 15 minutes left in the boil. Cool wort to around 70°F (21°C).

VARIATION

J2 Belgian Triple

"My sister's upcoming wedding inspired this variant."

Substitute White Labs' WLP500 Monastery Yeast to make a Belgian-style tripel.

VARIATION

Creave Saison

"I brewed this for the wedding of my friends Craig and Meave."
Reduce the starting gravity to 1.055; add Meyer lemon peel and
coriander to the fermenter; substitute a percentage of sugar for wheat;
and try French saison yeast for a summertime saison.

VARIATION

American Stowaway

"Interesting, drinkable, and unique."
Brew the same recipe as Creave Saison (above), but swap out the classic
German and French hops for new-school IPA hops, such as Simcoe and
Citra to the tune of 40 IBUs.

THE HOP PACK

It's an IPA world, and we're drinking it up. Meet the homebrewers who add an extra handful of hops to every brew.

NO BEER STYLE HAS HIJACKED THE hearts, minds, and stomachs of modern drinkers quite like the chameleonic India pale ale. It's pungent and bitter, hazy and tropical, citrus-spiked or smoother than soft-serve ice cream, equal parts shape-shifter and missionary, offering an eternity of flavor. Today's drinkers worship hops as an almighty deity.

The IPA was conceived in eighteenth-century England and saved from its deathbed in late-twentieth-century America, where the bitter style was reborn as a Molotov cocktail to mainstream lagers, anarchic punk to telephone-hold soft rock. IPAs were held aloft as symbols of flavorful expression, caustic tools to shatter long-held notions of good taste. The style was both powerfully flavored and a powerful concept that, like any trend in our interconnected global web, fast went viral worldwide.

The IPA is now uprooted from any geographic moorings, brewed anywhere and everywhere hops are sold. The newfangled Northeast IPA, foggy in hue and fruity in flavor, is homebrewed in Anchorage and Japan alike with no vast difference in deliciousness. Travel down to Argentinean Patagonia, and you'll find homebrewed IPAs hit with South American hops, while in South Korea you'll find Belgian IPAs brewed by an Italian homebrew shop owner—who learned to make beer in Australia.

Hop along as we explore the IPA diaspora.

ADAM BEAUCHAMP

BASKET RANGE, SOUTH AUSTRALIA

Adam Beauchamp's salt-of-the-earth family has tended the same property for more than 160 years. Today they grow the cherries and apples that occasionally go into his homebrew batches. His grandfather made apple wine and kit beers. "That it could be done at home interested me," says Beauchamp. So did saving money. He bought high-cost hop-smacked American IPAs from Green Flash and Stone but wanted to make something similar for less money.

Beauchamp built a bare-bones setup: wort boiled on the stove, a cooler that drains into a couple of pots. More than a decade later, he still averages around five gallons per batch, filling vessels with properly styled IPAs, pale ales, ambers, and malty lagers. "I focus on fresh ingredients, correct fermentation temps, good yeast health, and sanitation"—the holy quartet of homebrewing. He sources hops from wherever he pleases, ordering Citra and British-inspired New Zealand malts online. "We get them fresher than if we use Maris Otter or Golden Promise," he says of the flavorful UK grains. Why not his native grains? "Australian malts, particularly the base malts, produce bland lagers. They're very low color and low character. Unless you want to make a watery lager, that's all they're good for."

Summer in South Australia isn't for the faint of heart. Temperatures often crest into triple digits, a hard climate for humans and microbes alike. Beauchamp can brew for only six or seven months a year. "It's just too hot here, and I don't have good enough temperature control."

He wrings his best from the remaining months, and his skill shows in the results. He's been named South Australia's best homebrewer multiple times, and he's taken home Australia's top homebrewing title. It's a testament to the triumph of resourcefulness over technology. "I do the wort production in the kitchen and the fermentation anywhere that there's a space, really." He cooks lagers in winter, fermenting them in the laundry room alongside a couple of bricks of ice.

That make-do approach has made him a winner. Breweries have released several of his recipes, including his oat porter. Wins are nice, of course, but he doesn't want to fashion ribbons and trophies into a ladder to the next level. "That might ruin a good hobby," he says.

With no next-step brewery in mind and months between brew days, Beauchamp has ample time to think through his coming batches. He hits the area bottle shop monthly for research and, in between cooking curries and barbecuing dinner for his daughter and twin sons, perfects his next great beer. Today, it's an American amber; tomorrow, it could be fruit from the family farm that he transforms into the fruit of his labors.

ADVICE

Pay attention to detail. "Everything I do, I plan it out before I do it. I make sure everything is clean. I ferment at the right temperature. I use healthy yeast."

BREWER SPOTLIGHT

In 1993, Bell's Brewery keg washer Rik Dellinger and friend Rob Skalla homebrewed an intensely grapefruit-y IPA for a birthday party. It contained exclusively Centennial hops, then new, and inspired Two Hearted Ale, Bell's top-selling beer. Today, Dellinger is Bell's brewing materials manager.

HOPPY AMERICAN AMBER
ADAM BEAUCHAMP

"American amber is one of my favorite beers to drink, and I brew several batches of this recipe each year. I developed this recipe over the past five years, with a few variations that work just as well. I have used Gladfield Toffee Malt in place of CaraRed and Cascade hops in place of Riwaka. Over the years, this beer has won a few awards, including first place in 2012 and 2015 in the Australian Amateur Brewing Competition. The recipe was also brewed in collaboration with Birbeck's Brewing Company, which released it as Mallerstang."

SIZE	5 gallons (18.9 L)
ORIGINAL GRAVITY	1.056
FINAL GRAVITY	1.014
IBU	42
SRM	17
ABV	5.5%

MALTS AND ADJUNCTS

8 pounds (3.5 kg) 2-Row Malt

2.25 pounds (1 kg) Weyermann Munich Malt II

11 ounces (300 g) Wheat Malt

11 ounces (300 g) Weyermann CaraBohemian

11 ounces (300 g) Weyermann CaraRed

11 ounces (300 g) Briess Victory Malt

1.5 ounces (50 g) Weyermann Carafa Special II (dehusked black malt)

HOPS (60-MINUTE BOIL)

0.85 ounce (24 g) Magnum (12% AA), 60 minutes

0.7 ounce (20 g) Citra (13% AA), 10 minutes

0.7 ounce (20 g) Riwaka (5% AA), 10 minutes

1 ounce (28 g) Citra, Flameout

1 ounce (28 g) Riwaka, Flameout

1.75 ounces (50 g) Citra, Dry hop 5 days

YEAST

1 package (1.5 L Starter) Wyeast 1318 London Ale III

NOTES

Mash Mash temperature, 154°F (68°C), 60 minutes

Brewing Cool wort to 64°F (18°C).

Fermenting Let rise to 68°F (20°C).

CHICAGO HOMEBREW ALCHEMISTS OF SUDS

CHICAGO, ILLINOIS

chaosbrewclub.net

David Williams and Erick "Iggy" Ignaczak had a problem common to city dwellers: not enough square footage to homebrew and store equipment. "Many people [in Chicago] live in apartments and don't have brewing space," Williams says. The friends brewed together in his backyard, but they wanted a more dedicated space for their hobby. In 2011, they rented space in the basement of an artists' cooperative, next to a guy making soap. They invited fellow brewers to set up shop alongside their operation. "David and I figured that a year later there would be like five or six dudes brewing in this basement," Ignaczak says. "By the time we were done with that first build-out, we already outgrew the space."

Chicago Homebrew Alchemists of Suds (C.H.A.O.S.), as the club became known, took over an old community center workshop before finding its forever home in an old garage. C.H.A.O.S. today is better equipped than many start-up breweries. The 2,000-square-foot industrial space features an automated grain mill, gas burners, dangling brew kettles and coolers, a temperature-controlled fermentation room, and a wooden bar for bending elbows. A communal win-win, the gear largely was donated. "The caveat," says Williams, "was, 'We'll let you store it, but you've got to let other people use it.' "

Members reserve brewing slots online. "It's almost the model of the gym," Williams says. "You come in, you use the equipment, and you leave." Better still, you don't have to worry about your inoculated wort. One of the toughest challenges for apartment brewing is temperature control. Radiators hiss hot. Windows leak icy air. Variability wreaks havoc on yeast health. At C.H.A.O.S., Williams says, "you're not sticking it in a closet and letting it get up to the high seventies. In that fermentation room, it sits at a nice cool 67 or 68 degrees."

C.H.A.O.S. helps people ferment beer and friendships. "You don't always have to leave at the end of brewing," says Williams. "You can have a beer with the guys and chew the fat." Members meet at the monthly Tuesday Brewsday for a communal brew day, and the club runs seasonal parties, such as Cerveza de Mayo and Stout and Chili Night, featuring a cook-off and dozens of homebrews.

In recent years, club members have gone pro, including founders of Chicago's Vice District Brewing and Marz Community Brewing, as well as Arclight Brewing, in Watervliet, Michigan. Williams now is head brewer at Horse Thief Hollow Brewpub. The not-for-profit status of C.H.A.O.S. keeps it orderly and enables it to run smoothly, allowing the founders to step back from day-to-day operations. High-ranking "alchemists" host

IF I EXPLODE
CALL 7-3 824 5492

classes, brew for club events, and help maintain the brewhouse. "Everyone chipped in in some way to make this a home for themselves," Ignaczak says. "Why stop at 'make my own beer' when you could 'make my own brew club'?"

The club truly encompasses everyone. "It has been a beautiful social experiment of sorts," says Ignaczak. Big-city living can be unforgiving at times. Strangers rarely say hello, but beer can break down those urban barriers. The brew kettle acts as the local water cooler. "At the end of the day, it serves a great purpose," Williams says. "It provides not only a place for people to brew but a place for friendships to blossom and grow."

ADVICE

"If you buy a bourbon barrel, that's 53 gallons," Williams says. "One person brewing 53 gallons on a small homebrew system, that's a lot of brewing. If you have a club and have other people who want to brew for a barrel, all of a sudden you get 10 or 11 people together, and everybody brews the same recipe, and you're filling up that barrel a lot quicker."

BREWER SPOTLIGHT

Friends Tom Sullivan and Paul Karns founded their own homebrew cooperative in a garage in Richmond, Virginia, in 2010. During Sunday brew sessions, they met former Cambridge Brewing Company brewer Kevin O'Leary, with whom they later founded Ardent Craft Ales. "Each of us had our own ideas of going pro, and we found we had a lot of ideas in common," Sullivan says, adding that "the whole is greater than the sum of its parts." Try their pleasantly spicy and acidic saison.

NEW ENGLAND IPA
C.H.A.O.S.

"We brew large batches of the New England IPA for Tuesday Brewsday and serve it on the keezer at the club. It's definitely a club favorite!"

SIZE	5 gallons (18.9 L)
ORIGINAL GRAVITY	1.074
FINAL GRAVITY	1.020
IBU	40
SRM	5
ABV	7%

MALTS AND ADJUNCTS

12 pounds (5.44 kg) Fawcett Pearl Malt

1 pound (0.45 kg) Flaked Oats

0.5 pound (0.23 kg) Sucrose

HOPS (90-MINUTE BOIL)

5 milliliters Hop Extract (60% AA), 60 minutes

1 ounce (28 g) Mosaic (11.6% AA), 1 minute

1 ounce (28 g) Galaxy (14.2% AA), 1 minute

1 ounce (28 g) Mosaic, Whirlpool

1 ounce (28 g) Galaxy, Whirlpool

2 ounces (56 g) Mosaic, Dry hop

2 ounces (56 g) Galaxy, Dry hop

YEAST

2 packages Omega Yeast Labs OYL-052 DIPA Ale or Wyeast 1318 London Ale III

NOTES

Water Profile (in PPM) Adjust water to Ca: 100, Cl: 35, SO_4: 110.

Mash Add lactic acid to achieve pH of 5.3.

Mash temperature, 152°F (67°C), 60 minutes

Brewing Add sucrose with 15 minutes left in the boil. Cool wort to 65°F (18°C).

Fermenting When gravity reaches 1.025, dry hop with 1 ounce (28 g) Mosaic and 1 ounce (28 g) Galaxy. Two days later, dry hop with another 1 ounce (28 g) Mosaic and 1 ounce (28 g) Galaxy. Another 2 days later, rack the beer into a keg.

Post-fermentation Do not age the beer. Drink it as quickly as possible.

ZOIGLHAUS BREWING

PORTLAND, OREGON
zoiglhaus.com

For more than five centuries, the subjects and citizens of Neuhaus, Eslarn, Falkenberg, Mitterteich, and Windischeschenbach—where Germany yields to Czechia—have filled steins with zoigl, a malt-forward lager produced at communal brewhouses. Locals take turns manning the wood-fired kettles, serving their unfiltered lagers at makeshift home bars signified by six-sided stars hanging outside.

"We really liked the idea of a communal brewhouse," says Alan Taylor, who visited the region with his wife. "We thought it would be great for Portland." In late 2015, Taylor, a veteran of various German-inspired breweries as well as Full Sail and Widmer, opened Zoiglhaus Brewing. It offers hefeweizens, kölsch, lagers, and an unusual opportunity: Customers can buy five gallons of pristine wort paired with a can of fresh Imperial Yeast. All of the homebrewing ingredients without the hours of hard work.

FUN FACT

Many breweries offer fresh wort to homebrewers for their fermentations. Nebraska Brewing runs the annual Wort Transformation Challenge; Bell's Brewery provides brewers with wort for its yearly homebrew competition; and Free State in Kansas and Little Fish in Ohio both supply homebrewers with the second runnings of strong barley wines and imperial stouts.

"You can come in with your carboy and be out in half an hour—and probably have a pint of beer while you're here," Taylor says. "You're making beer in the time it takes you to get home." Six weeks later, homebrewers come back to share their beers. "Not a single beer tastes the same," says Taylor, who uses the tastings as inspiration. For example, folks adulterated a German-inspired pale ale with honeydew melons, lager yeast, and souring bacteria. "Homebrewers are notorious for creativity. They don't think like a professional brewer, and that's not necessarily a bad thing."

Getting the government to license the concept took finessing, however. Taylor originally wanted to offer inoculated wort, a federal no-no. "They said, 'You can't do that because it's alcohol.' I said, 'No, it's not.' They said, 'Yes, it is.' I said, 'Trust me, there's less alcohol in that after 24 hours than orange juice.' They said, 'As soon as you inoculate it with yeast, we can't control how much alcohol is in it.' "

The law also prohibits Portland residents from running pop-up home bars, but Taylor sees his program as a faithful representation of the zoigl concept, underscoring brewing's communal nature and creating a level playing field for novices and hardcore homebrewers alike. The best part is that batches are basically foolproof. "If you come in and you have a clean carboy and a clean airlock, and I fill it with clean wort, and you pitch clean yeast, the chances of you not screwing it up have gone down so much already. Most professional brewers were all homebrewers at one point, so we have a soft spot in our heart for homebrewers."

EMMA CHRISTENSEN

SAN JOSE, CALIFORNIA
emmachristensenmedia.com

Emma Christensen is equally at home fermenting a dry-hopped double IPA, blueberry-lavender mead, or kombucha cut with honey and green tea and has worked hard over the last decade to become one of homebrewing's brightest stars.

She went to college to study physics before majoring in creative writing. That left brain–right brain balance pays dividends on brew days. "You kind of need this analytical side where you're like, 'I'm going to make a chocolate porter,'" she says. "You research, create your initial recipe, and make it. Then you're like, 'OK, that was a pretty good chocolate porter. How can I make it better?' At the same time, you're bringing in this creative side like, 'Well, that was a great chocolate porter, but what if we did a Mexican chocolate porter?'"

Christensen fell under brewing's spell while living in Boston, where she attended the Cambridge School of Culinary Arts. Friends invited her over for a brew day, introducing her to a new world. "It was crazy to me that it was possible. I got bit by the bug."

She and husband, Scott, eventually moved to Columbus, Ohio, where she bought a Mr. Beer kit. "It was disgusting," she says of her initial batch. "But there was something about the process, that sciencey, alchemy thing that hooked me. I kind of got a glimmer in that first failed experiment that it could be awesome." The couple brewed together, tension simmering between them like a brew kettle. "Some of the worst arguments we've ever had have been about brewing beer."

Like marriage, the early days of brewing brim with uncertainty. "You read the directions, and it seems clear, but then you get into the kitchen and you're like, 'What does that mean? What does *rolling boil* actually mean? Is *this* a rolling boil?'" Writers write what they know, so she pitched a publisher a memoir about learning to navigate brewing and marriage.

That proposal was shot down, but it started the conversation with a publisher that led to *True Brews*, the first of her three books to date. Christensen learned valuable lessons while assembling the book and honing its recipes. "If you give people the basic one, two, three, four, five steps to create a fermented beverage, they can do anything. Your strawberry soda might not be the same as my strawberry soda, and your porter might not be the same as my porter, but they're both still delicious. We both followed the same steps and ended up with something tasty."

She wrote her follow-up, *Brew Better Beer*, in an 800-square-foot apartment in the San Francisco Bay Area. She brewed almost daily, hiding beer behind doors, in the bedroom, in cupboards, and even outside. "Because it doesn't get super-cold in California, I had

stuff chilling on our balcony until I could get to it. It was super intense, super hard, and there's a steep learning curve, but after a while I just felt like I got it. I understood how, if I made this little change, I'd understand exactly what would happen."

FUN FACT ──────────────

Homebrewers founded San Francisco's Black Sands Brewery, a multipurpose venue that offers coffee, cocktails, and house-made beer, plus the ingredients and equipment needed to make them at home, including five-gallon recipes for the beers on tap. Check them out at blacksandsbeer.com.

─────────────────────────

Brewing, she says, is like studying a foreign language. The best learning technique is immersion. Repetition breeds understanding and confidence. Stumbles become successes. The process becomes second nature. "There are so many parts of the brewing process that are not in our day-to-day life. You don't know what bubbling is and whether that's good or bad. We don't have a context for that, so you have to take a deep breath and learn from the process. You're not going to know everything going into it."

ADVICE

"The first time you step into a kitchen to brew your own batch of beer, it's going to feel stressful and crazy. Just be prepared for that and know that your first batch might not be amazing. Have reasonable expectations. Take your first, second, and third batches as learning experiences and trust that every time you brew you will learn a little more. Some things are going to stop feeling so scary and will feel more natural. It's a learning process, and you have to let yourself be in that learning process."

BREWER SPOTLIGHT

Former Army officer Kevin Inglin and his wife, Shea, run San Francisco's Ferment Drink Repeat, a combination homebrew shop and brewery that pours frequent collaborations with area amateur brewers.

HAPPY HOPPY WEST COAST PILSNER
EMMA CHRISTENSEN

"I developed this recipe early on while writing *Brew Better Beer* but ended up cutting it from the final manuscript. I'm very happy to rescue it from the discard pile and finally share it! This pilsner is German at heart but West Coast in its hoppy attitude—though not so much that you'll confuse it for an IPA. Be sure to use a temperature-controlled fridge during fermentation so you get that clean and crisp character of a true pilsner."

SIZE	5 gallons (18.9 L)
ORIGINAL GRAVITY	1.047
FINAL GRAVITY	1.009
IBU	41
SRM	5
ABV	5%

MALTS AND ADJUNCTS

7.5 pounds (3.40 kg) German Pilsner Malt

1.25 pounds (0.57 kg) Vienna Malt

0.5 ounce (14 g) Black Patent Malt

1 teaspoon (5 g) Irish moss

HOPS (90-MINUTE BOIL)

1 ounce (28 g) Cluster (6.8% AA), 90 minutes

0.75 ounce (21 g) Mt. Hood (6% AA), 30 minutes

0.75 ounce (21 g) Mt. Hood, Flameout

YEAST

1 Package (2 L Starter) White Labs WLP830 German Lager

NOTES

Mash Mash temperature, 148°F (64°C), 60 minutes

Mash out temperature, 170°F (77°C), 5 minutes

Sparge temperature, 170°F (77°C)

Brewing Add Irish moss with 30 minutes left in the boil. Cool wort to less than 75°F (24°C).

Fermenting Ferment at 50°F (10°C) for at least 2 weeks and up to 4 weeks. Raise temperature to 60°F (16°C). Transfer to a sanitized carboy and lager for 1 to 3 months at 40°F (4°C).

STEFANO DALLA GASSA

SEOUL, SOUTH KOREA
SeoulHomebrew.com

Before beer came leather and grapes. Stefano Dalla Gassa's father owned a tannery and vineyard, and they made wine together. The younger Dalla Gassa started homebrewing in Australia, but the scorching climate proved prohibitive. "I couldn't make a proper beer," he says. Dalla Gassa and his wife later moved to Seoul, where he worked as a leather craftsman for a fashion company. He loved his new life. The lagers, not so much. "Korean beer is really flavorless," he says.

Then Dalla Gassa got sick. It was the kind of all-consuming illness that devours entire days. He visited a doctor and discovered that he had an allergy to certain preservatives. Dalla Gassa stopped drinking Korean beer, and his malady rapidly vanished. "I thought, *Oh my god, I have some problem with alcohol*," he recalls.

FUN FACT

South Koreans consume more liquor per capita than any other country. The average citizen consumes around 14 shots per week, more than double the amount of the average Russian, next on the list.

He returned to his native Italy, feasting on his family's homemade cheese, bread, wine, and beer that his dad had brewed. "I didn't get sick," he says, deciding that Korean beer was the culprit. At the time, mass-market Korean beer was light-bodied and bubbly, perhaps laced with adjuncts such as corn and rice. The lagers were mostly forgettable but had a huge fan base, because they made a great match with the country's spicy, strongly flavored cuisine and barbecue. "When I drank Korean beer, it tasted like there was something missing in its flavor and body." His solution: homebrew.

After his diagnosis, he frequented Seoul's only homebrew shop, but the owner was planning on selling it and leaving the country for good. Would the store shut down if he couldn't find a buyer? "I told him, 'I'm going to buy it off you and see how it goes.'"

He cut costs by dealing directly with Italian equipment manufacturers—more reliable than Chinese gear, he says—stocked in-demand hot hops, such as New Zealand's Nelson Sauvin, and created ingredient kits for house recipes such as a Trappist-inspired porter. "Now I make a living out of this, and I can have my beer and not get sick."

That's how an Italian native, who learned English in Australia—where he met his Korean wife—came to helm Seoul Homebrew, which functions as more than just a supply depot. Dalla Gassa serves as a soothsayer, counseling customers by call, text, or WhatsApp. "People ask me, 'Can you give me a recipe for New England IPA?'" he says, noting that his best-selling yeast strain is Wyeast London Ale III, instrumental in creating Heady Topper,

The Alchemist's famed hazy IPA. "I'm trying to help them, step by step, so they get the confidence. Koreans don't always have a lot of confidence when they start something they don't know. They don't want to take a risk. They think, *If I get into this hobby and fail, I'm going to throw away all this money.* I take them from crawling to walking and running."

As in other megalopolises, Seoul homebrewers deal with a space crunch. Here, instead of brewing in tiny apartments, many people go to brewing labs that provide everything from equipment to fermenting rooms for a small fee. Dalla Gassa teaches hands-on classes at cost. For him, the mission is more important than the money. "We want to show people that, after all, making beer at home is not so difficult. At the end of the day, my question is, 'Have I made somebody happier today?' My answer is always yes."

Happiness comes in waves, and South Korean culture runs on trends. Pale ales were popular, then IPAs, and then sours. "Now there's a trend going on that, when you get married, you commission a microbrewery to make your own homebrew with a label on it. During the ceremony, you distribute the bottles of beer to the people."

Fads come, fads go. Dalla Gassa wants to create a generation of self-assured homebrewers who are in it for the long haul. "If I can give more people self-confidence, eventually they'll come back and start brewing themselves and then, who knows? Maybe one day they set up a microbrewery."

ADVICE

"No matter how appealing it is, never start with a cheap kit. Homebrewers, they start making beer with a prehopped kit like Cooper's. It's not so bad, but there's an abyss between starting there and extract. They come to me and say, 'I started making beer with this one, but it's not very similar to the beer I'm drinking in a pub. It has no body, it has no character, no feeling when I drink it.' I walk them through the next step."

BREWER SPOTLIGHT

Korean-American homebrewer and former Microsoft employee Bryan Do founded the Hand and Malt Brewery near Seoul. It runs South Korea's largest hop farm, provides yeast to local bakeries, and makes beer such as the K Weisse, soured with *Lactobacillus* bacteria isolated from local kimchi.

BELGIAN IPA
STEFANO DALLA GASSA

"I made this recipe with the intention of trying Mangrove Jack's Belgian yeast strain. I also like IPAs, so I wanted to create some hybrid that could work well together. The yeast produces a significant amount of fruity esters. The East Kent Golding hops have spicy aromas and a slightly citrus taste, so they blend well. Even though the final gravity is very low, the beer is not dry at all. With long aging, the beer tends to lose its aroma, but it acquires different notes of dried fruits, like plums and cherries. Every month I open a bottle and taste something new. This beer never stops surprising me."

SIZE	5 gallons (18.9 L)
ORIGINAL GRAVITY	1.056
FINAL GRAVITY	1.004
IBU	48
SRM	7
ABV	6.8%

MALTS

5.5 pounds (2.5 kg) 2-Row Malt

1.1 pounds (0.5 kg) Rye Malt

1.1 pounds (0.5 kg) White Wheat Malt

1.1 pounds (0.5 kg) Maris Otter Malt

0.85 pound (0.4 kg) Castle Château Abbey Malt

HOPS (60-MINUTE BOIL)

2 ounces (56 g) Willamette (4.5% AA), 60 minutes

1 ounce (28 g) East Kent Golding (4.5% AA), 60 minutes

1 ounce (28 g) Willamette, 20 minutes

1 ounce (28 g) East Kent Golding, Flameout (steep 45 minutes)

1 ounce (28 g) East Kent Golding, Dry hop 7 days

YEAST

1 package Mangrove Jack's M-41 Belgian Ale

NOTES

Mash Mash in temperature, 129°F (54°C), 15 minutes

Mash temperature, 149°F (65°C), 45 minutes

Mash out temperature, 172°F (78°C), 15 minutes

Fermenting Ferment at 71°F (22°C) for 3 weeks.

Post-fermentation Bottle condition for six weeks at 75°F (24°C.)

SIX BREWERIES THAT STARTED AS HOMEBREW SHOPS

Ballast Point

In San Diego in 1992, Jack White created Home Brew Mart, the launch pad for Ballast Point. Homebrewer Yuseff Cherney joined as the first employee, and many of the brewery's best-known beers—Sculpin IPA, Grunion Pale Ale—began as amateur experiments. The Homework Series, released under the Home Brew Mart brand, features recipes printed on the label.

Bell's Brewery

In 1993, Larry Bell founded the Kalamazoo Brewing Co. homebrew-supply shop. Two years later, Bell's used a 15-gallon soup kettle to cook up batches of beers, including the herbal, toasty Amber Ale, which the company still produces today.

Final Gravity Brewing Co.

In Richmond, Virginia, visit the Original Gravity homebrew shop to stock up on grains and hops before heading to the adjoining Final Gravity to try nearly a dozen beers brewed on a two-barrel system, including the Irish Goodbye Foreign Extra Stout and Venus Rising Double IPA.

Kuhnhenn Brewing Co.

Brothers Bret and Eric Kuhnhenn took over their dad's hardware store and started selling homebrew supplies. Hops replaced hammers, and their Michigan brewery debuted in 2001. Drink their DRIPA, a double IPA dried out with rice.

Listermann Brewing Co.

Cincinnati couple Dan and Sue Listermann went into business handmaking homebrew equipment (lauter tuns) in 1991. Dan bought a used two-barrel system in 2008, and Listermann Brewing was born. Nutcase Peanut Butter Porter is their must-sip.

Two Brothers Artisan Brewing Company

Jim and Jason Ebel opened the Brewer's Coop in 1993 before spinning off Two Brothers in 1996. Their grandfather, a retired dairy farmer, donated dairy tanks, which served as the original fermenters.

RAMIRO DE DIEGO

FENRIS
SAN MARTÍN DE LOS ANDES, ARGENTINA

I n this craggy land of glacial lakes, near the Chilean border, pumas prowl the forested Lanín National Park, from which rises an ice-capped dormant volcano. It's a natural paradise—just not for homebrewers like Ramiro de Diego.

"When I started brewing, I was really isolated. I was the only homebrewer that I knew," he says. "I live 1,600 kilometers from Buenos Aires, where everything happens." But the Internet can shrink vast expanses. De Diego went online and lapped up all the information Google and Amazon offered.

The local water was soft and pristine, easily adaptable to most styles. He made Scottish ales, golden ales, IPAs. In time, the student soon became the master, and in 2015 Somos Cerveceros, Argentina's national homebrewing association, named de Diego homebrewer of the year. Consider it proof that, when it comes to brewing, sometimes simplicity is best.

"I'm not the kind of homebrewer who has a complicated setup," says de Diego. For five or six years, he made do with a five-gallon stainless steel pot and a camping cooler as a mash tun. No muss, no fuss. "Getting the equipment to be really simple allows you to control everything better. It's very simple to clean."

In 2014, the graphic designer combined a couple of buildings in his front yard, tiled the walls, and dug floor drains to fashion Fenris, a nanobrewery that turns out

80 gallons of beer at a go. "It's a very small setup," he says. "I do everything. I work alone. I don't expect to grow any bigger." De Diego fills and cleans every keg himself—in addition to raising his two daughters.

Brewing in Patagonia has its drawbacks and advantages. He has access mainly to dry yeast, which limits the styles he can produce. Then again, he lives only a couple of hours from El Bolsón, a huge region for Argentinean hop production.

FUN FACT

In the Southern Hemisphere, the hop harvest happens in February. El Bolsón hosts El Lúpulo al Palo, a festival featuring technical presentations, plenty of hopped-up beer, and loads of grilled lamb, a traditional Patagonian feast. In March, the city also hosts the annual Fiesta Nacional del Lúpulo, a cultural celebration featuring beer, music, and a hop queen contest.

The region grows varieties at once familiar and foreign, like the local Cascade. "It's quite different. It has a really strong grapefruit character, and it's not as floral as U.S. Cascade." Another prominent native hop is the fruity, citric Mapuche, which de Diego uses in brown ales.

FUN FACT

Belgium's Leffe Royale uses a range of globetrotting hops, including a spicy, fruity version made with Mapuche.

De Diego uses exclusively El Bolsón hops in his well-balanced IPA Argenta. "It doesn't have a rough bitterness," he says of his most popular offering at Crux Cervecería, the local bar where he sells most of his beer. (Fenris doesn't have a taproom.) His regular production releases include American IPAs, oatmeal stouts, Scottish ales, and an annual wet-hopped ale flavored with hops from his own garden.

Commercial brewing is all about repetition and consistency rather than wild trials. "It's more limiting," says de Diego, who still conducts small-batch trials, monkeying around with barley wines, Belgian witbiers, imperial stouts, and barrel aging. "Homebrewing is the best way to experiment and really experience every style. Even if you start doing this commercially, you should never stop homebrewing."

ADVICE

- "Patience is an ingredient in brewing, and sometimes there's not enough."
- "Make it simple. Don't get complicated with the setup. Use contests and homebrewing partners to get feedback about what you're doing. It should be a tool for you, a resource to know if you're doing things right and how to improve what you're doing. Competitions are a very useful tool that not many home-brewers use."

BREWER SPOTLIGHT

"In the late sixties when I started brewing, there was almost no knowledge available," says Sierra Nevada founder Ken Grossman, who opened the Home Brew Shop in Chico, California, in 1976. Sierra Nevada's paradigmatic Pale Ale started as a homebrew, and Grossman honed the recipes over the course of dozens of batches. "The basic tenets of our early homebrew pale ale are the same. We used the same yeast we were using as homebrewers. We've refined our pale ale, but we haven't changed the process."

IPA ARGENTA
RAMIRO DE DIEGO

"This IPA is brewed with 100 percent Argentinean hops from El Bolsón. Most of these hops have a bold, citrusy, fruity character. The recipe was developed in 2013 during meetings for Somos Cerveceros, which is Argentina's national homebrewing association."

SIZE	5 gallons (18.9 L)
ORIGINAL GRAVITY	1.060
FINAL GRAVITY	1.012
IBU	62.9
SRM	11
ABV	6.3%

MALTS AND ADJUNCTS

8.31 pounds (3.77 kg) Pilsner Malt (1.8°L)

1.08 pounds (0.49 kg) Munich Malt (9°L)

0.55 pound (0.25 kg) Weyermann Carahell Malt

0.55 pound (0.25 kg) White Wheat Malt (2.4°L)

0.33 pound (0.15 kg) Briess Carapils

HOPS (90-MINUTE BOIL)

0.46 ounce (13 g) Nugget (15% AA), First Wort (90 minutes)

0.25 ounce (7 g) Victoria (11% AA), 30 minutes

0.35 ounce (10 g) Cascade (10% AA), 15 minutes

0.25 ounce (7 g) Bullion (12% AA), 15 minutes

0.35 ounce (10 g) Cascade, 5 minutes

0.35 ounce (10 g) Bullion, Whirlpool (steep 30 minutes)

0.35 ounce (10 g) Cascade, Whirlpool (steep 30 minutes)

2.82 ounces (80 g) Cascade, Dry hop 3-4 days

YEAST

1 package Fermentis SafAle US-05 Dry Yeast

NOTES

Mash Mash temperature, 153°F (67°C), 60 minutes

Sparge temperature, 168°F (76°C)

Fermenting Ferment at 64°F (18°C).

DEVILCRAFT

―――○―――

TOKYO, JAPAN
en.devilcraft.jp

Japan's homebrewing laws are fuzzier than a kitten. Creating wort and adding hops are perfectly acceptable. But add yeast and you're breaking the law. Why? The legal threshold is 1% ABV. "I'm always wondering, *When does it become illegal?*" says Tokyo brewer Mike Grant. "No one knows when it's over 1 percent or under 1 percent. Generally people don't have labs in their houses to measure the alcohol."

FUN FACT ――――――――――――――――

For its low-ABV Go To IPA, Stone Brewing took its inspiration from San Diego Session Ale, a collaboration between Ballast Point and homebrewer Kelsey McNair, who has since opened North Park Beer Co., which makes the dankly fruity Hop-Fu!.

――――――――――――――――――――

"Because of the strict homebrewing laws, no one wants the attention that being in a book would garner," wrote Lee Reeve, owner-operator of the Abrewcadabrew homebrew club (page 140). Which explains why I hit a brick wall in my hunt for a Japanese homebrewer. "It's not just the Japanese, either. None of the foreign homebrewers want to dance with the tax office devils here."

"There's a fear among people who are homebrewing because they're holding out that hope about going pro," Grant says. "We don't have to worry about that anymore."

"We" means Grant, John Chambers, and Jason Koehler. The trio cofounded Tokyo-based DevilCraft, a collection of craft beer bars fueled by a brewery with homebrew roots. These American expats, who boast more than 30 years of combined homebrewing experience, met in Tokyo as part of a subterranean scene with one eye on the law and the other on making better beer by any means necessary. "Because it's not legalized here, it hasn't become popular," Grant says. "It's not a hobby or a thing. In the States, everybody knows someone who homebrews. To the general population in Japan, it's basically unknown or underground."

DevilCraft does well by pale ales and orange vanilla porters, imperial stouts and imperial IPAs—all in line with the founders' stateside upbringing. Grant grew up around San Francisco before jetting to Japan to teach. On a visit home, Grant's younger brother introduced him to homebrewing. "I was hooked as soon as I did one batch," says Grant, who immediately ordered homebrewing equipment and brought it back to Japan.

He stuffed school vacations with brew sessions and ordered ingredients from afar. Today Japan has several online brew shops, but shipping sacks of grain is prohibitively expensive, so he visited a local brewery and asked to buy malt.

"What are you going to do with it?" they asked.

"Just leave that to me," Grant replied. "Of course, they figured it out, but eventually they sold me a bag of malt."

The clandestine homebrew community led him to his two business partners. DevilCraft, which debuted in 2011, started as a pub serving Chicago-style deep-dish pizza and good commercial beer. However, the 50-year-old building couldn't bear the load of heavy brewing equipment, an architect said, exercising caution in the wake of that year's catastrophic Tōhoku earthquake and tsunami. Plan B entailed installing a brewing system in a second location, but they ran into a good problem: too many customers. "We didn't want to take out 20 seats because that was our cash flow," Grant says.

Luckily, they found a nearby building where they could place their preordered brewhouse—if it ever arrived. The system languished in the quicksand of customs for nearly a year. "There was no brewing going on, except at home," says Grant. Japan has strict food sanitation laws, and a lab must test anything that touches a food product. "Each test is about $1,000. Of course, there were hundreds of gaskets, and each one would have to be tested individually. It got a little bit ridiculous."

By September 2015, the homebrewers reached the end of their multiyear odyssey and began brewing professionally. "There's no impetus to change the law," says Grant, who still homebrews occasionally to test DevilCraft recipes. "I don't see it happening. That's unfortunate because, the way the scene grew up in the States, there was almost no delineation between craft and homebrew. If you tell someone who is not familiar with the process what homebrewing is, they're like, 'Isn't it dangerous?' Well, is making soup dangerous? People have no clue that it's an age-old tradition that's been lost."

ADVICE

- Brew a ton. "At my peak, I was brewing almost every week. Yeast is awesome that way. It's ready in a week to be used again."
- "Yuzu and mikan are so complementary to hop flavors, but you have to have a light touch. They tend to get heavy-handed pretty quickly."
- "You need to talk to your yeast. You have to understand your yeast. Keep your yeast happy, and you'll be happy. To me, that's the biggest thing that unlocks consistency and quality over time. If you can take care of one strain of yeast over several generations, you're going to make several clean beers. Yeast is king."

BREWER SPOTLIGHT

Japan's Ichiri Fujiura won America's Homebrewer of the Year award in 1998 thanks to his visionary Toasted Coconut Porter. He returned home not to accolades but to a government warning to knock it off. Today, he runs Tokyo's Watering Hole beer bar.

DEVIL JUICE SIPA
Session IPA
DEVILCRAFT

"This is a great beer. Moderate in alcohol and light in body, Devil Juice is crushable in quantities and still lets you keep your wits. The winning combination of Citra and Simcoe hops, with Waimea thrown in for a unique twist, will satisfy any unquenchable thirst for hoppiness. *Kanpai!*"

SIZE	5 gallons (18.9 L)
ORIGINAL GRAVITY	1.045
FINAL GRAVITY	1.014
IBU	46
SRM	7
ABV	4.1%

MALTS AND ADJUNCTS

7.7 pounds (3.5 kg) 2-Row Malt

14 ounces (400 g) Briess Carapils

8.8 ounces (250 g) Caramel Malt (40°L)

8.8 ounces (250 g) Weyermann Melanoidin Malt

8.8 ounces (250 g) Flaked Oats

HOPS (60-MINUTE BOIL)

0.7 ounce (20 g) Simcoe (13% AA), 60 minutes

0.35 ounce (10 g) Amarillo (9.2% AA), Flameout (steep 15 minutes)

0.35 ounce (10 g) Simcoe, Flameout (steep 15 minutes)

0.35 ounce (10 g) Waimea (17.5% AA), Flameout (steep 15 minutes)

1 ounce (28 g) Amarillo, Dry hop 3 days

1 ounce (28 g) Citra (12% AA), Dry hop 3 days

1 ounce (28 g) Simcoe, Dry hop 3 days

1 ounce (28 g) Waimea, Dry hop 3 days

YEAST

1 package Wyeast 1056 American Ale

NOTES

Mash Mash temperature, 158°F (70°C), 45 minutes

Mash out temperature, 168°F (75.6°C), 10 minutes

Post-fermentation Carbonate to 2.3 volumes of CO_2.

VARIATION

Mash high (158°F [70°C]) and try adding 1 percent lactose to add a little more body.

ABREWCADABREW

YOKOHAMA, JAPAN
abrewcadabrew.com

Connecting homebrewers in a country where the act is illegal requires organizational magic. Abrewcadabrew's mission is to become a center for Japan's far-flung homebrewers. They sell equipment and starter kits, sure, but the club also arranges educational talks, clandestine bottle-shares, beer events at restaurants and bars, and brew-on-premise pop-ups and workshops.

"I've created a network of locations where I've got kitchens, I've got space, and no one gets in trouble—well, not yet," says Abrewcadabrew founder Lee Reeve.

The Glaswegian fell into homebrewing in 2009, when social networking was still in its infancy. "I wanted this community, and I couldn't find it," says the writer and graphic designer. So he started a blog and named it Abrewcadabrew after his twin passions: magic and beer. Like ants to honey, Japanese homebrewers slowly found the blog. "It became a hub," says Reeve, who started arranging real-world meet-ups. Maintaining a website is hard work, though, and the blog slowly fizzed out.

In 2016, Reeve was sitting at a bar, eavesdropping on a conversation about homebrewing and Japanese beer. "It just dawned on me: Why not create a club?" He rebranded and relaunched Abrewcadabrew later that year, attracting natives and expats alike.

"Homebrewing law is the stigma of everything in Japan," he acknowledges. "Because it sounds so threatening, there are homebrewers who will refuse to do anything on a public level because they fear that the taxman will come knocking on their door and take everything away."

Reeve remains undaunted, however. "I'm trying to create a one-stop-for-all community for homebrewers in Japan."

BRIAN HALL

ANCHORAGE, ALASKA

Brewing merges art and discipline, and Brian Hall had the latter locked down. He earned his master's degree in education, later teaching math, Earth science, and applied engineering. He started homebrewing in summer 2003 while living in Fairbanks, Alaska, in a dry cabin—meaning no running water. He and a friend settled on a hard apple ale and raspberry wheat, warming the beer with an aquarium heater. "The raspberry beer ended up tasting really hammy, and the apple ale almost tasted like Coors Light. We called it the Bronze Bullet. I didn't know what I was doing."

In Anchorage, he dived headlong into a 15-gallon all-grain system, tinkering with his techniques and cardamom-spiced Belgian dark ales—"a perfect blend of cooking, art, and science."

His wife's med-school studies brought the family to Maine, where he toted along one brew kettle and two kegs. "I was like, 'Maybe I'll brew a little bit.' But the scene there was huge, and I went bonkers." He worked on Sebago Brewing's bottling line and drew inspiration from Portland breweries such as Bissell Brothers, experts in the hazy New England–style IPA, and Allagash, a 20-minute bike ride from his house. The latter brewery inspired him to experiment with wild, sour, and spontaneous ferments, but his trials met with error. "Mine were chilling down far too quickly. You want 12 to 16 hours, and mine were cooling off in about half that." He started harvesting bottle dregs during tastings and deployed them in his

own sours, blending batches to create alchemy. "It's kind of like tuning a guitar," he explains. "With a guitar, if you're off by a tiny bit, it'll sound terrible. But blending has a bit more margin for error."

Hall and his wife moved from Maine back to Alaska with two kids and a staggering amount of alcohol. "They charged me by volume and not weight, so instead of bringing back empty kegs I brought back full kegs. Most homebrewers would invite friends and neighbors to empty the taps, but Hall's kegs and carboys contained precious cargo. He'd spent years painstakingly cultivating a collection of long-aged sours and wild ales in the vein of Belgian lambics and gueuze. "I'm stupidly nostalgic for tucking something away for a long period of time and pulling out a dusty bottle years later," he says. "We brought back 7,000 pounds, of which one-third was beer and wooden barrels."

Back in Anchorage, Hall has resumed his brewing schedule, which he split into two sizes and philosophies. He brews on a 55-gallon system to create his wild ales, which nap in wooden casks. He also cooks up five-gallon batches on his stovetop, a manageable proposition while watching his kids. "The pursuit of perfection in all that I craft has begun to consume me as I get older," says Hall, who also bakes bread. (He's kept the same sourdough starter alive for nearly a decade.)

He forages for local ingredients, such as juniper and blueberries, endlessly refines his recipes and techniques, and shares his knowledge, most notably in seminars at America's annual National Homebrewers Conference. "Having previously been a teacher, I really enjoy educating people on how to make beer and in practices that are efficient. When I make a lambic-style beer or

New England–style beer, I think it's something I can easily explain to someone else."

Hall wants to open a wood-fired brewpub specializing in his three passions: bread, butter, and beer. Like his liquids, the project is following its own timeline. "I like the idea of having something that takes time to create."

ADVICE

"Don't be afraid to try new things. Just because someone has told you that something has been done a certain way for 20 years, you should try it a different way. At the homebrew level, there's no reason we should be emulating professional brewers."

BREWER SPOTLIGHT

Denver homebrewer Sean Buchan ditched his physical therapy career to cofound Cerebral Brewing, where he makes electrifyingly aromatic New England–style IPAs such as Drone Uprising and Secret Chat Room, inspired by techniques he perfected at home. "While I was homebrewing, well before our opening, I was fortunate enough to receive a few beers from The Alchemist and Hill Farmstead from a friend out east. They completely changed my perception of what IPAs could be, and I set out to learn everything I could about them. I focused on huge whirlpool hop loads and excessive dry hopping, while incorporating more protein-heavy malts into the grain bill to boost body."

ALOHOPS
New England IPA
BRIAN HALL

"Late-hop additions have been my jam lately. I've been trying out different methods, trying to figure out what makes the New England IPA the New England IPA. If you want something simpler than all the whirlpool additions, I also find one larger addition works just fine."

SIZE	5 gallons (18.9 L)
ORIGINAL GRAVITY	1.068
FINAL GRAVITY	1.013
IBU	59
SRM	5
ABV	7.1%

MALTS AND ADJUNCTS

5 pounds (2.3 kg) 2-Row Malt

5 pounds (2.3 kg) Maris Otter malt

3 pounds (1.4 kg) Flaked Oats

3 pounds (1.4 kg) Pilsner Malt

1 pound (0.45 kg) Lactose

HOPS (60-MINUTE BOIL)

0.4 ounce (11 g) Magnum (14% AA), 60 minutes

0.5 ounce (14 g) Mandarina Bavaria (8.5% AA), Whirlpool (steep 30 minutes)

0.25 ounce (7 g) Citra (12% AA), Whirlpool (steep 30 minutes)

0.25 ounce (7 g) Mosaic (12.5% AA), Whirlpool (steep 30 minutes)

1 ounce (28 g) Mandarina Bavaria, Whirlpool (steep 20 minutes)

0.5 ounce (14 g) Citra, Whirlpool (steep 20 minutes)

0.5 ounce (14 g) Mosaic, Whirlpool (steep 20 minutes)

1.5 ounces (42 g) Mandarina Bavaria, Whirlpool (steep 10 minutes)

0.75 ounce (21 g) Citra, Whirlpool (steep 10 minutes)

0.75 ounce (21 g) Mosaic, Whirlpool (steep 10 minutes)

0.5 ounce (14 g) Mandarina Bavaria, Dry hop high krausen

0.25 ounce (7 g) Citra, Dry hop high krausen

0.25 ounce (7 g) Mosaic, Dry hop high krausen

0.5 ounce (14 g) Mandarina Bavaria, Dry hop post-fermentation

0.25 ounce (7 g) Citra, Dry hop post-fermentation

0.25 ounce (7 g) Mosaic, Dry hop post-fermentation

1 ounce (28 g) Mandarina Bavaria, Dry hop in keg

0.5 ounce (14 g) Citra, Dry hop in keg

0.5 ounce (14 g) Mosaic, Dry hop in keg

YEAST

2 packages or 2 L Starter Wyeast 1318 London Ale III

NOTES

Water Profile (in PPM) Adjust water to Ca: 124, Mg: 5, Na: 14, Cl: 150, SO_4: 100.

Mash Mash temperature, 150°F (66°C), 75 minutes
Sparge temperature, 168°F (75°C)

Brewing Add lactose with 15 minutes left in the boil. After boil, chill wort to 185°F (85°C), then hold it for whirlpool.

Fermenting Start dry hopping at high krausen. If not kegging, add final dry hop 4 days before packaging.

Post-fermentation Carbonate to 2.3 volumes CO_2.

CALLISTER BREWING

VANCOUVER, BRITISH COLUMBIA
callisterbrewing.com

Brew enough beers in your backyard or kitchen, and at some point you'll probably think: *I should start a brewery.* It's a great daydream, but opening one requires dump trucks of bucks.

Spouses Chris Lay and Diana McKenze started off brewing five-gallon kits in their one-bedroom apartment. The hobby snowballed, and thoughts turned—of course— to going pro. "The British Columbia marketplace was starting to get a little crowded, and we realized that a new brewery needed a niche," says Lay, a digital media entrepreneur. So, over the course of a year and a half, they founded Callister Brewing, a brand-development program for homebrewers pondering the professional leap without having to break the bank.

"It really solidified this idea that, if there was a way to make and sell the beer while going through this process, that would be great," Lay recalls. Renting space to breweries also relieves the pressure of brewing Callister beers—such as Exhibition Rye IPA and Blossom Dearie dry-hopped grisette—to pay the bills. "We are a very small entity. I am not only head brewer but also head of marketing and head of janitorial duties."

Each year, the roughly four-barrel brewery welcomes a trio of fledgling breweries for one-year stints, including cloudy-IPA experts Superflux and English specialist Real Cask. Callister's setup is completely hands-on, and brewers gain immediate access to the brewing equipment.

"The rents here in Vancouver are high, and a brewhouse will set you back half a million dollars," says Kent Courtice, who built a local reputation for bang-up IPAs and sours brewed with friends Ryan Seller and Phil Spurgeon under

callister brewing co.

1338
franklin
street

the Boombox Brewing umbrella. Courtice, Seller, and Spurgeon wanted to give it a shot, so they teamed up with Callister. "It's the only place where you can have that opportunity," Courtice says. "To be able to go in and start brewing professionally is phenomenal."

Everything produced at the facility—including pilot batches—is sold at the on-site taproom, where brewers take turns tending the bar. "If somebody really wants to know something, there's a brewer nearby," Lay says.

Face-to-face interactions build relationships and provide unfiltered feedback. "It's one thing drinking and enjoying your beer, but having other people try your beer is important," says Courtice. "You can have 40 people come in, and they're only there because they want to try your beer. You can't put a price on that."

Callister's program offers a low-risk chance to homebrewers who want to explore the professional waters. "We did make some big mistakes," Courtice says, alluding to a shower of coconut beer, "but I'd rather make a mistake at 500 liters than 5,000 liters."

If the sea proves too choppy, you can always return to safe harbor in your kitchen. But if it's smooth sailing, then maybe a bigger adventure awaits. Boombox plans to build on its early success by outsourcing production to another brewery while it funds and builds its permanent home. "You learn not only how to brew on a larger scale but also how to source ingredients," says Courtice. "It's been a one-year education. It was phenomenal."

BREWER SPOTLIGHT

VanBrewers, Vancouver's preeminent homebrew club, serves as a feeder system for the city's professional scene. Graham With founded the organization in 2009, later becoming brewmaster at Parallel 49 Brewing, where he makes famed beers, including Salty Scot, a Scottish wee heavy sprinkled with sea salt.

DENNY NEILSON

— ◦ —

THE WINEMAKER
JERUSALEM, ISRAEL
thewinemaker.co.il

enny Neilson's wife dreamed of moving to Israel. The clock, however, was ticking. "Once you get past 50, if you have a dream, you'd better get busy," Neilson says. So they sold their Tennessee farm, packed up their possessions, and schlepped their three children to Jerusalem. "We made *aliyah*," he says, using the Hebrew word for far-flung Jews settling in Israel.

In the land of milk and honey, he found precious little beer, however, just a couple of forgettable local brews, Guinness, and Heineken. "There were literally about five beers available commercially," he says.

In 2005, Neilson founded the Winemaker, a shop specializing in home wine kits sourced from Canada and Italy. Trouble was, the government considered the kits food products and nixed their importation, a massively expensive lesson. "There are so many grapes available in Israel that importing wine kits was pretty stupid." He ditched grapes for grains and started Israel's first homebrew store in his suburban garage.

Neilson didn't brew much back in Tennessee, but in Israel he hurled himself headlong into his new career. "Back in the early days, it was try it and pour it out if it didn't work."

"He's going to be modest about this," interjects his son, Matt. "He's probably read every book on homebrew that ever existed. He's got those hands where everything turns to gold. For him, it was pretty easy."

"They call me the grandfather of Israel's beer industry," says the elder Neilson. The Winemaker pollinated Israel's burgeoning brew scene, offering ingredients, homemade rigs, and instructions to a country lacking in all three. When he moved there, zero independent breweries operated in the nation. Since then, many of his former students have opened commercial breweries, including Lone Tree, Shapira, and Ronen. "We kind of helped launch the industry."

Neilson and son now professionally produce more than a dozen fermented beverages: spirits, the Buster's brand of hard ciders, boozy lemonades, and beers that include a brisk pilsner and an oak-aged stout. His best-known brew is the Chutzpah Double IPA (page 160), inspired by Russian River's Pliny the Elder.

"Most Israelis don't know what hops are," Denny laments. "At beer festivals, our Chutzpah sign says, EXTREMELY HOPPY. They go, 'What are hops?' I go, 'Have a cider.'"

With classes in English and Hebrew, the Winemaker attracts a diverse range of customers young and old, religious and secular. At least half of the customers don't know what beer to make. "He'll say, 'Don't worry about

it. You're going to make beer. What do you like?'" Matt says of watching his dad in action. "They might not even know what they like. It's up to him to put together a good first recipe. It's giving them a security net to make them confident."

Many request wheat beer because distributors do a bang-up job marketing Weihenstephan in Israel, says Matt. IPAs and stronger stuff soon follow because Israel has exorbitant alcohol taxes and a beer can easily cost 35 shekels (more than $10). No wonder the average bar patron buys only one beer. Commercial breweries are heeding the market and cranking ABVs to 9, 10, 11%— double the digits, double the fun.

"That's just not where we are," Denny says. In the Winemaker taproom, you'll wade through lower-ABV waters. "Our concept is the social aspect of drinking, not the drunkenness of drinking."

Some months are lean, others fat, but father and son remain optimistic. Customers come, customers go, some come back. "It's a much more expensive hobby here than in America," says Denny. "A very small percentage of people get serious about it." Those who do embrace the native landscape by spiking beers with silan—a date-derived syrup that boosts ABV and flavor—and subbing wild sage for hops. Israel now has four homebrew shops and more than 30 native brands of beer. Those numbers look even more impressive when you realize that Israel has a population of about 8 million people and half of them don't drink.

"How many people move to Israel for economic opportunity?" muses Denny. Opening a new market requires a healthy dose of self-confidence, but brewing is a higher calling for the Neilson clan. (As far as Neilson knows, the Winemaker is Israel's only business to hold licenses for wine, beer, and liquor.) "Our purpose goes beyond finances. I kind of equate our continued business for our reason for making *aliyah*. If you move to Israel and don't move back, you're successful."

ADVICE

Start with a simple recipe, then add flavors and ideas. "I tell people to start basic and then say, 'Do you want it sweeter? Stronger? Weaker? Lighter? How do you want to change it?'"

BREWER SPOTLIGHT

After retiring from the Israeli air force, pilot and longtime homebrewer Ori Sagy founded Israel's Alexander Brewery. It uses water from the Sea of Galilee in its range of beers, including the bière de garde–inspired Ambrée and the floral, Belgian-style Blonde.

CHUTZPAH
Double IPA
DENNY NEILSON

"We call our favorite homebrew Chutzpah. It is a double IPA with a very rich body. It's surprisingly not too bitter, with tons of hop flavor and aroma. When you taste it, you'll know why we named the beer. Wow! That's some kind of chutzpah."

SIZE	5 gallons (18.9 L)
ORIGINAL GRAVITY	1.082
FINAL GRAVITY	1.016
IBU	130
SRM	6
ABV	8.9%

MALTS AND ADJUNCTS

11 pounds (5 kg) 2-Row Pale Malt
0.5 pound (0.45 kg) CaraMunich II
0.5 pound (0.45 kg) Briess Carapils
0.5 pound (0.45 kg) Dextrose

HOPS (60-MINUTE BOIL)

2 ounces (56 g) Chinook (12% AA), 60 minutes
1 ounce (28 g) Columbus (14% AA), 30 minutes
2 ounces (56 g) Centennial (10.5% AA), 10 minutes
2 ounces (56 g) Simcoe (13% AA), 2 minutes
1 ounce (28 g) Centennial, Dry hop 10 days
1 ounce (28 g) Columbus, Dry hop 10 days
1 ounce (28 g) Simcoe, Dry hop 10 days
0.25 ounce (7 g) Centennial, Dry hop 15 days
0.25 ounce (7 g) Columbus, Dry hop 15 days
0.25 ounce (7 g) Simcoe, Dry hop 15 days

YEAST

2 packages Wyeast 1056 American Ale

NOTES

Mash Mash temperature, 150°F (65°C), 60 minutes
Sparge temperature, 170°F (77°C)

Fermenting Ferment at 70°F (20°C) for 10 days.

Post-fermentation Keg or bottle 3 days after last dry hop addition.

THE FUNKY BUNCH

These brewers go wild for feral yeast and souring bacteria
that'll bring a pucker and smile to your lips.

OOK AT THE GROUND. LOOK UP IN THE
air. Look at your hair. Everywhere you
stare you'll find yeast, the microscopic
munchers that crunch the sugars in wort
and convert them into alcohol. Most brewers,
amateurs and pros alike, make beer with lab-grown
strains of impeccable purity. Cook up the ideal
climate, measure the correct ratio of grains, add
the hops at just the right time, and yeast will
reward you with the desired fragrance, taste, and
alcohol level. Lather, rinse, repeat.

There's comfort in knowing exactly how microbes
will behave, as obedient as the family dog. But some
brewers like to live on the wild side. They find fun
in *Brettanomyces*, a genetically diverse clan of wild
yeast that boogies to its own unpredictable beat.

Some strains create fragrances of pineapple and
mango, while other varieties can be funkier than a
Kool & the Gang concert. Beginner and professional
brewers have taken an increasing shine to wild
yeast's thrilling variance and potential for new
flavors.

Upstart yeast labs (page 188) now offer a range
of rare and unusual wild strains and bespoke blends,
often incorporating souring bacteria. Homebrewers
have taken fermentation into their own hands,
harvesting microbes from fields of flowers and fruit
orchards. In Tennessee, you'll find Belgian-inspired
lambics as complex as anything in Brussels, while
New Zealand–grown plums supply a tart Berliner
weisse with a Southern Hemisphere twist.

Let's bug out.

CHRIS ALLEN

ONES & ZEROS BREWING CO.
NASHVILLE, TENNESSEE
onesandzerosbrewing.com

Ever since he was 12 or 13 years old, Chris Allen has fiddled with computers and technology. He relishes building synthesizers from scratch and dropping beats as a DJ and VJ, creating large video installations and massive lighting shows that offer a sideline from his day job as a technology director for a private school, where he doubles as the head coach of the robotics team. "Every year since I've started it, we've been Tennessee state champions," says Allen.

So it's no surprise that Allen has transformed half of his home garage, built into a hill, into a stainless-steel temple to the intersection between automation and fermentation. A massive freezer contains six half-barrel kegs converted into brite tanks, essentially a lagering cellar on steroids. "We call it the Cryo Chamber," he says. He ripped open the guts of a couple of glass-door refrigerators, bypassing internal thermostats and converting them into fermentation chambers. "I can hold temperature inside of the thermal well within a tenth of a degree and ramp up or ramp down. It's had an extremely positive impact on my beers."

FUN FACT

Allen achieves his lab-precise temperature control with a BrewPi Spark (brewpi.com), a sensor and controller that requires hacking into a fridge to install a heater and controlling the compressor.

Allen wasn't his family's first homebrewer, though. He and his wife bought her father a kit for Christmas, and dad and daughter brewed together on the kitchen stovetop for about a year and a half. "I was always the one designing bottle labels for them," says Allen. Eventually, he grew tired of watching. "I just said, 'I'm going to do it myself.' Then I basically took it to the extreme." Allen sold his music studio to buy homebrew equipment, gradually piecing together his tricked-out system and brewing ethos.

In 2016 alone, his competition haul included six best of show awards, 17 gold medals, 12 silver, and 5 bronze. ("I've got so many medals that I quit counting.") His brewing repertoire includes German pilsners, Goses, Märzens, raspberry lambics, and wee heavies, each a paradigm of its kind. "When I set my mind to something, I go for it with full force. I'm a total perfectionist. The beer must be perfect to me. Competing is just a way to verify that I'm brewing to a classic style."

The keys to his success are fermentation control, evading oxidation, and the infinite pursuit of improvement. "Perfection to me would be seeing a beer go from taking bronze medals to gold medals to best of shows." That kind of dedication means lots of brewing and comparatively little imbibing. "I don't drink much of my beer. Now it's more about, 'How long can I lager this thing?' I'm definitely the kind of guy who's going to brew it, take my time, and not rush it."

Nor is he rushing to go pro. "So many of my friends are like, 'When are you going to open your new brewery?' Not tomorrow." Allen foresees opening a brewery maybe sometime in the next decade. "I would love to find a way to brew great beer but not be so reliant that it's your sole source of income." For now, he shares beers with friends and his local club, Music City Brewers, finely calibrating his garage operation. "I'm trying to invent new ways to push the scope of homebrewing."

ADVICE

"Typically, I do 12-gallon batches. That's 12 gallons of finished beer. I always make the batches slightly larger, assuming that I can lose a couple gallons to get the right end process."

BREWER SPOTLIGHT

Michael Crane was never much of a beer drinker, either. He started brewing to spend more time with his sons, and in time he became one of the Midwest's best homebrewers, using offbeat ingredients such as beets, matzo, and harvested wild yeast. He turned his unexpected talent into Missouri's Crane Brewing, which focuses on lambics, saisons, and sours such as the Beet Weiss.

RASPBERRY LAMBIC
CHRIS ALLEN

"This lambic-style sour is perfectly tart, with subtle notes of raspberries and barnyard. Don't be alarmed by the pink color! The key to the beer's success is the Belgian lambic yeast. This beer gets better with age, so try to ignore it for at least 12 months."

SIZE	5 gallons (18.9 L)
ORIGINAL GRAVITY	1.064
FINAL GRAVITY	1.002
IBU	7
SRM	10
ABV	7%

MALTS AND ADJUNCTS
5.4 pounds (2.45 kg) Weyermann Floor-Malted Bohemian Pilsner Malt
4.2 pounds (1.91 kg) Light Wheat Malt
0.4 pound (0.18 kg) Flaked Wheat
0.8 pound (0.36 kg) Candi Sugar

HOPS (90-MINUTE BOIL)
0.4 ounce (11 g) Saaz (4% AA), 60 minutes
0.4 ounce (11 g) Saaz, 10 minutes

YEAST
3 packages Wyeast 3278 Belgian Lambic Blend

NOTES
Mash   Mash temperature, 156°F (69°C), 90 minutes
Mash out temperature, 168°F (76°C), 10 minutes
Sparge temperature, 168°F (76°C)

Brewing   Add candi sugar with 10 minutes remaining in the boil.

Fermenting   Ferment at 68°F (20°C) for 30 days. Rack to secondary carboy. Age for a year and a half with 1.75 pounds (0.8 kilograms) of raspberry puree.

Post-fermentation
Bottle condition.

MITCH GRITTMAN

HALF HEARTED BREWING CO.
NEW ORLEANS, LOUISIANA
halfheartedbrewing.com

While attending culinary school in Minnesota, Mitch Grittman began homebrewing as a passing hobby in order to make cheap beer. He worked as a chef for a spell before returning to college. "My love for brewing and the science behind it drew me away from cooking and into food science," he says. After a pit stop in Chicago, where his beer obsession ballooned, he and his wife moved to New Orleans. He began doing R&D for a food manufacturer, specializing in frozen liquid foods. "We made basically anything that could be pumped through a pipe."

New Orleans pulls its water from the Mississippi River, which courses more than 2,000 miles across America. Dozens of variables impact its chemical makeup, including snowmelt in Minnesota and farm runoff in Missouri. "I tested the pH in my water one day," says Grittman, "and it was 9.0 because there was so much chloramine in there. We're one of the oldest cities in the United States, and our infrastructure matches that. A couple of times a year we get a boil advisory because the municipal advisory company can't confirm that the water is safe to drink."

Alcohol can kill just about anything, except creativity. Grittman, who cut his brewing teeth on the pristine waters of the Land of 10,000 Lakes, doubled down on making dynamic local beer. The most obvious route—tapping into the Big Easy's venerated culinary scene—proved unappetizing. "We've got a lot of great food ingredients, but red beans and gumbo don't slide into beer so well." He took another avenue to terroir: capturing and cultivating wild yeast.

FUN FACT

Some yeast strains favor heat, while others prefer cooler weather. Push a strain outside its comfort zone, and it'll unleash off flavors, such as rotten eggs. Kviek (pronounced *kwike*) is happy as a clam anywhere from 70 to 100 degrees Fahrenheit. Norwegians traditionally store strains on dried linen, woven straw rings, or "yeast logs" dotted with drilled holes and use it to produce farmhouse ales. American labs such as Yeast Bay have begun propagating and selling kveik to homebrewers and professional brewers alike.

Grittman turned one of his home's three bedrooms into the headquarters for Half Hearted Brewing Co., a brewery-in-planning specializing in American sour and wild ales. Tempered by blackberries, Black Oak open-ferments in an oak cask, with ambient Louisiana microbes turning the beer wildly acidic. Five strains of *Brettanomyces* intertwine in Hype-P-A, while tropical hops infuse it with their aromas. Gobs of passion fruit and guava flavor the tart Hialeah Jack Berliner weisse, a fruity refresher suited for the city's sweltering climate. "In the summertime, I do a lot of low-ABV fruited sours with tropical fruits."

Insulated from wall to wall, windows covered, and cooled to a steady 60 degrees with a modified 240-volt air conditioner, the dedicated brew room teems with carboys, a chest freezer, and refrigerators. Grittman plugged any air leaks and latched the door to ensure a tight seal. "It's been a work in progress, like all beer projects," he laughs. His attention to detail takes its roots from the New Orleans climate and its potentially ruinous impact on beer. "When I first came down here, I made a couple batches of vinegar—not on purpose. I was living in a shotgun house where hot air was blowing through cracks in the floor." (The combination of spontaneous fermentation and high humidity caused a fair amount of mold.)

"Beer brought me into my career, and my career has accentuated the beer that I brew at home," he says of his role as product developer at Smoothie King, where he develops novel flavor and fruit combinations. Half Hearted—the name a carryover from his days brewing with plastic buckets—forms part of the tightly stitched, still emerging homebrew scene in New Orleans. "All the beer nerds in a sea of cocktails and drive-through daiquiri places, we huddled together for warmth."

A strong and supportive homebrew community accelerated Grittman's growth as a brewer, as have his facility and comfort with reading and comprehending brewing journals. "There's a ton of information out there that is unattainable to the average homebrewer just because of the jargon."

While plotting Half Hearted's next steps, Grittman is raising his profile by collaborating with local breweries such as Wayward Owl, where his wife works, and judging brewing competitions, where he doles out practical knowledge that helps homebrewers improve their fermentation game.

ADVICE

"You can learn malts pretty easily. You can learn hops pretty easily. You can learn what yeast needs. But water, as simple an ingredient as it is, is the most complicated. That's why people say, 'Don't think about water right now. Get back to water later.' Too many people don't take it seriously when they first start to brew, and they never come back to it. I was kicking myself when I finally took the time to really understand water. Don't disregard water. I've heard and read in books, 'If the water tastes fine, then go with it.' I've come to a point in my brewing career where I couldn't think anything is less true than that. Brewing water is the most important ingredient that you have. Learning about the chemistry will take you from an amateur homebrewer to an advanced homebrewer."

BREWER SPOTLIGHT

Mixed-fermentation master Michael Tonsmeire and fellow homebrewer Scott Janish, an IPA specialist, are planning to open Sapwood Cellars in Maryland, focusing on barrel-aged and fresh, hop-forward ales.

AMERICAN MIXED-FERMENTATION FARMHOUSE-STYLE SAISON

MITCH GRITTMAN

"Choosing your primary yeast has a profound impact on your finished flavor. An estery primary yeast gives you fruitier flavors, while a phenolic yeast provides more funk. Aging the beer in a corny keg with an adjustable pressure relief valve means no airlock, no oxygen, and you can sample with a party tap instead of a siphon. This recipe will give you a slightly tart, slightly funky farmhouse-type saison. I always brew a double batch and split the beer into two vessels. One will have a short boil and be drawn off before the hops are added. It receives a big dose of collected mixed culture. That beer will acidify heavily and won't have much character; the second batch provides the bulk of the flavor. Blending is the key to a quality mixed-fermentation beer."

SIZE	5 gallons (18.9 L)
ORIGINAL GRAVITY	1.052
FINAL GRAVITY	1.000
IBU	11
SRM	4
ABV	6.2%

MALTS AND ADJUNCTS

7 pounds (3.175 kg) Belgian Pilsner Malt

1.75 pounds (0.79 kg) Flaked Oats

1.25 pounds (110 g) Flaked Wheat

0.3 pound (99 g) Aromatic Malt

HOPS (60-MINUTE BOIL)

0.5 ounce (14 g) East Kent Golding (5% AA), 60 minutes

0.5 ounce (14 g) Saaz (2% AA), 20 minutes

YEAST

1 vial The Yeast Bay Wallonian Farmhouse

1 vial The Yeast Bay Saison Blend

Bottle Dregs or Wild-Capture Mixed Culture*

* "I buy sterilized 50-milliliter centrifuge tubes from Amazon and collect bottle dregs at bottle shares. That's a reliable way to collect bacteria and *Brettanomyces* that has produced a proven beer."

NOTES

Mash Mash temperature, 155°F (68°C), 60 minutes

Fermenting Ferment with the saison and farmhouse yeasts until
terminal gravity has almost been achieved (around 1 week). Rack into
secondary with mixed culture and age until final gravity is stable for
around 2 months. If blending an acid beer, age the final blend until final
gravity is stable for around 2 months.

PAUL HOBSON & LARA MURPHY

DURHAM, NORTH CAROLINA

facebook.com/modernromancebrewery

High school romances rarely survive graduation, a hazard of young love that Lara Murphy and Paul Hobson know all too well. The North Carolina couple dated for a couple of years, but the relationship crumbled when the elder Hobson left for college. Their lives then took them on separate roads. Murphy moved to New York City, and Hobson married and took off to Texas. Divorce brought him back to Durham, though, where Murphy also had returned. They reconnected and rekindled their romance over cold brews.

"We'd make dinner together, I'd bring a favorite beer, and he'd bring a favorite beer to the next dinner to share," Murphy says.

"Early on in those days, we had a sense of what beer we liked, but we didn't know beer," says Hobson. "I couldn't look at a shelf and tell you the difference between a kölsch and a pilsner, or a pale ale and an IPA. It became a two-way obsession."

Love deepened with each passing beer, and within a year the couple married, honeymooning in Belgium. Drinking and traveling deepened their beer knowledge, and then Hobson, a meticulous medical editor, had a revelation: "If you really want to know beer truly and intimately, you have to start making it," he says. Murphy bought him a homebrew kit for Christmas.

That marked the first blush of Modern Romance, the couple's brewery-in-planning. "We wanted it to feel like us," says Murphy. "We wanted it to be about our relationship and also how we feel about beer. It was about cultivating our love of craft beer, our love of brewing, and our love of each other. We fell in love with all that stuff simultaneously."

Over the last five years, Hobson and Murphy have brewed through the global style guide: snappy Czech pilsners, German Märzens, Belgian tripels, salt-licked Goses, robust porters, wild IPAs, peppery saisons. You name it, and the twosome has brewed it, named it, and labeled it. "I was making labels for batch four because I'm a crazy person," admits Murphy, who has a background in marketing.

Initially their beer was rough as sandpaper, though. "We were using kits with questionable ingredients," she says. "We were super-inexperienced, and our technique was terrible. We were doing it on our stove instead of a nice burner. We were just winging it." They joined the local Nash Street Homebrew Club (which they later ran). Experienced brewers' advice proved essential to their growth. "Sometimes on the homebrew forums, someone could sound like an ultimate authority, but you've never had their beer, and you don't know if you should trust them. They're also invisible," says Murphy. "To get feedback from your local homebrew community is invaluable."

They watched as fellow homebrewers went pro, paying close attention to the start-up process, discussing

how they'd do things differently. Speculation became Modern Romance's business plan. They found a space in downtown Durham in 2015, the same year that Murphy found a lump in her breast. Cancer has a nasty habit of putting dreams on hold, but sickness also brings out the best in the tight-knit beer world.

"All those friends we made through homebrewing and the North Carolina beer community were the ones bringing me to chemo when Paul was out of town, making us meals, and helping take care of our pets," Murphy says. "It was such a rough year. The community really rallied around us, and it was all due to beer."

With Murphy's breast cancer in remission, the couple re-embraced Modern Romance. They're searching for a new space in Durham and, like every married couple, have decided what roles each person will play. "Our teamwork aspect naturally lends itself to running a business," Murphy says. "Paul is going to run back of house, and I'm going to run front of house. I'm a marketing professional, and he's a killer on the recipes. It's a really nice fit. If I were hiring someone, I'd hire Paul, but we happen to be married."

ADVICE

- "As a basic point, especially for a novice brewer, don't be afraid to fail," says Hobson. "Worst-case scenario: You'll dump it out and try again. That's usually the first thing I'd say. The second thing is, 70 percent of what you're doing as a brewer is cleaning and sanitizing, and if you do that, your chances of making good beer are pretty good."

- Hobson advises, "Just think about what you want the beer to taste like. Don't worry about the ingredients. Just worry about the experience you want with the beer in your glass. You can go from there and engineer backward. The best way to start is, 'What do I want to drink?'"

BREWER SPOTLIGHT

Longtime friends and amateur bicycle racers Rob Kolb and Anthony Accardi loved collecting unique yeast, wild and tamed, which they set loose in their rustic homebrews. Their hobby became Transmitter Brewing, a farmhouse-inspired brewery in New York City. Seek out anything in their F series of *Brettanomyces*-fermented beers.

BRETT IPA
PAUL HOBSON & LARA MURPHY

"We love the character *Brettanomyces lambicus* gives when used for primary fermentation. It suggests hay and leather when you smell it but gives off a great pear/pineapple flavor with just a little bit of that drying, phenolic, funky snap. Then you put Citra or Mosaic in it, and, well . . ."

SIZE	5.5 gallons (20.8 L)
ORIGINAL GRAVITY	1.060
FINAL GRAVITY	1.008
IBU	45
SRM	4
ABV	6.8%

MALTS AND ADJUNCTS

9.1 pounds (4.1 kg) Pale Malt

2.8 pounds (1.3 kg) White Wheat Malt

0.5 pound (226 g) Acidulated Malt

0.5 pound (226 g) Briess Carapils

HOPS (60-MINUTE BOIL)

1.15 ounces (32 g) Chinook (13% AA), 60 minutes

3.5 ounces (99 g) Citra (12% AA), Flameout (steep 30 minutes)

3.5 ounces (99 g) Cascade (5.5% AA), Flameout (steep 30 minutes)

3.0 ounces (85 g) Citra, Dry hop 3 days

2.0 ounces (56 g) Cascade, Dry hop 3 days

3.0 ounces (85 g) Mosaic (12.5% AA), Dry hop 3 days

YEAST

40.5 ounces (1,200 ml) Starter White Labs WLP653 *Brettanomyces lambicus*

NOTES

Water Profile (in parts per million) Adjust water to Ca: 90, Mg: 15, Na: 64, SO_4: 178, Cl: 102, HCO_3: 104

Mash Mash temperature, 151°F (66°C), 60 minutes

Mash out temperature, 168°F (75°C), 15 minutes

Brewing At the end of the boil, cycle the hot wort through a plate chiller and back into the kettle until the base temperature in the kettle falls below 170°F (76°C). Then start the 30-minute whirlpool rest.

Fermenting Ferment at 72°F (22°C) for 12 to 14 days.

BOOTLEG BIOLOGY BUGS OUT

Jeff Mello was fed up. Working as a fundraiser for Washington, D.C., nonprofits was fulfilling, but work was a slog. "He was coming home and dreading going to work the next day," his wife, Erin, recalls. He had started homebrewing, though. "The more I brewed, the more I realized that it was my passion," he recalls. "So I quit."

After reading an article about lambic starters, Mello filled three mason jars with wort, crowned them with cheesecloth, and placed the yeast feast in his garden. Then he put the jars in a closet. "When I looked at them a few months later, they were completely nasty," he says. The first jar smelled like creamed corn. The second had grown something mushroomy. The third one smelled like . . . honey? "It had promise," says Mello, who brewed with the yeast, which resulted in a cross between a saison and a spicy hefeweizen, something familiar yet thrillingly new. He named the strain *S. arlingtonensis*, after his backyard in Arlington, Virginia, and pondered the microverse surrounding him. "If I could get yeast that made pretty good beer from my backyard, where else could I get them?"

In 2013, that curiosity became Bootleg Biology, an open-source endeavor to obtain and isolate microbes from free-range sources such as flowers, kimchi, walnuts, yogurt, bottle dregs, and even spruce berries from a Colorado amusement park. "You can buy pure brewer's yeast cultures, but I wanted to show people that you can source yeast from anywhere," says Mello, who now lives in Nashville. "Yeast provides a sense of place."

To underscore that idea, he launched the Local Yeast Project to amass the world's most diverse bank of microbes, one from every American ZIP code. Since the Postal Service has approximately 43,000 codes—"I looked

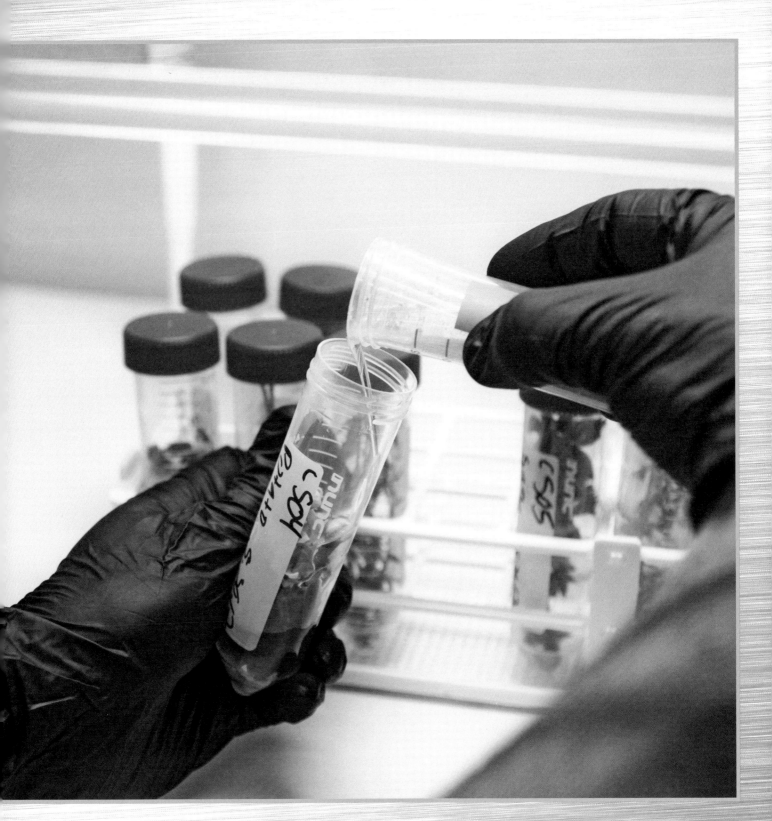

up the number once and decided that I'd never think about it again"—Mello needed help. "I thought, *If I'm going to make this project successful, then I really need to focus on teaching people to harvest yeast.*"

To his surprise, culturing yeast proved pretty simple. "You can buy agar at international food stores, and Petri dishes are just plastic plates," he explains. To empower other brewers, he designed the Backyard Yeast Wrangling Tool Kit, which contains all the tubes, pipettes, and sterile swabs necessary to capture wild yeast. When someone isolates a strain, he or she plops a cultured swab into a prepaid envelope and mails it to Mello, who deposits it in his bank.

"The kit was a great idea, but it's not the end goal. The goal was to create a yeast company." Over the last couple of years, Bootleg Biology has started selling homebrew and commercial strains, including Sour Weapon, isolated from Nashville-area flowers; the Funk Weapon series of *Brettanomyces* cultures; and a saison blend curated by homebrew legend Michael Tonsmeire, better known as the Mad Fermentationist. Bootleg Biology also does quality control for local breweries, testing beers' bitterness, checking for contamination, and banking yeast and bacteria in their laboratory-grade freezer. "We want to do all the things that we think are exciting at the same time," Mello says. "I never want to be just a yeast factory."

SIX UPSTART YEAST LABS

East Coast Yeast

New Jersey microbiologist Al Buck focuses on reviving forgotten yeast strains and a wide range of wild blends.
TRY ECY10 Old Newark Ale, reportedly the house strain for Ballantine Ale, which was produced in Newark.

Escarpment Laboratories

Two Ontario college students turned their yeast-harvesting hobby into a business supplying Canadian brewers and homebrewers with strains, such as the fruity Foggy London Ale.
TRY Ontario Farmhouse Ale Blend, which contains yeast isolated from native strawberries and *Brettanomyces* strains sourced from Ontario wine barrels.

Imperial Yeast

This Portland, Oregon, company produces more than 25 strains of USDA-certified organic yeast, uniquely packaged in cans.
TRY W15 Suburban Brett. Dark fruit is this strain's dominant attribute, ideal for wood-aged beers.

Inland Island Yeast Laboratories

Denver friends John Giarratano and Matthew Peetz grew industrial-scale yeast for the biofuel industry before launching this start-up that sells scores of strains from sake to Oregon IPA.
TRY INIS-903 Brettanomyces Bruxellensis III, isolated from a Belgian brewery, delivers huge gusts of tropical fruit.

Omega Yeast Labs

Founder Lance Shaner uses his 16 years of homebrewing experience, plus a PhD in molecular genetics and microbiology, at his Chicago-based lab that sells yeast suited for fruity IPAs and funky wild beers alike.
TRY Saisonstein's Monster, their homegrown hybrid of French and Belgian saison strains that creates a strong, spicy farmhouse ale with tartness and a touch of bubble gum.

The Yeast Bay

Bio-scientist Nick Impellitteri founded this Bay Area lab that has supplied brewers with award-winning strains, including Funktown Pale Ale and Wallonian Farmhouse.
TRY Amalgamation, a blend of six *Brettanomyces* strains, produces a bright, kindling-dry beer with a multifaceted fruit flavor.

JAMIE MCQUILLAN

CELL DIVISION
DUNEDIN, NEW ZEALAND

Fruit complements farmhouse ales and sour beers better than anything else," says Jamie McQuillan, who grew up on an orchard, with the scent of fresh, ripe apples and pears accompanied by fallen produce's rotting, fermented funk.

At the 2016 Society of Beer Advocates National Homebrew Competition, New Zealand's premier contest, McQuillan won both top brewer and top beer for a Berliner weisse fermented with wild *Brettanomyces* yeast and greengage plums. He parlayed that triumph into a nanobrewery that garbles the line between amateur and professional.

In most places worldwide, brewing and selling beer requires a non-residential dwelling, even something as simple as a backyard shed. Following the letter of New Zealand law, McQuillan has a license to brew, age, and sell his fruited sours from the comfort of his kitchen.

Compared to today's gleaming, plug-and-play systems, his setup is old-school. He uses his mother's vintage canning equipment to heat his water, then ferments in a shelved hot-water cupboard—a storage space typically built around a water heater or boiler—positioning his beer at different heights. The higher the positioning, the higher the temperatures. "I don't believe a fancy kit makes a better brewer; it's all about good process," he says.

A neuroscientist researching Parkinson's disease and meticulously following sterility protocols, McQuillan perfected his airtight methodology. "There's *Brett* everywhere in my house, I'm sure, but it doesn't crop up where I don't want it. I have to remind myself that I'm not actually working in a tissue-culture lab." His day job, along with a guitar hobby, informed his brewery's snappy name: Cell Division riffs on English post-punk band Joy Division.

McQuillan didn't know whether his skills would amount to much, though. "I was brewing over-the-top hop water," he says of his early forays into pale ales and IPAs. But he sharpened his talents by entering competitions and absorbing feedback, not all of it positive. "The first time I entered the nationals was after a year of brewing. That was really rough."

As with science, the minutiae mattered most. He began paying attention to the composition of his water and brewing robust yeast starters, extensively recording every step and evaluating the beer's evolution. "I can look back on them and troubleshoot." Those details soon paid dividends on the medal stage and led to overseas research at American sour specialists such as Upright and the Rare Barrel.

McQuillan doesn't plan to quit his day job, which offers a safety net for him to continue messing around with saisons and long-aged sours on a small scale. He experiments with locally grown apricots, plums, raspberries, and quince shipped from his family's orchard. He assesses his successful cultures, harvesting his favorite microbes, and freezes them for long-term storage. "In New Zealand, we don't have any yeast production facilities, so it's a little tricky getting fresh yeast," he says.

Cell Division is a passion project that never need multiply, but at the same time it can become a means to an end. "I've started this crazy idea of brewing my beer commercially on a very small scale at home."

ADVICE

"I listen to feedback from national competition judges and people who drink a lot of good beer and have honest opinions, especially my partner. Learning to evaluate your own beer subjectively is equally important. I also try to take something from each brew forward to the next one, always improving."

BREWER SPOTLIGHT

In 2016, Christian DeBenedetti went from writing about homebrewing to owning Wolves & People Farmhouse Brewery in the Willamette Valley of Oregon. The operation sits on his family's 21-acre hazelnut farm, where he plucked wild yeast from the property's plum trees.

JEALOUS PLUMS BERLINER WEISSE

JAMIE MCQUILLAN

"Jealous Plums began as a no-boil Berliner weisse using the methodology in Michael Tonsmeire's *American Sour Beers*. My personal blend of *Lactobacillus* resulted in an approachable level of sour with a pH of 3.5. I then aged this beer on greengage plums with *Brettanomyces*, transforming it into a wild specialty beer with a relatively short maturation time. The final result is a beer with light funk that integrates well with the fruit and moderate acidity."

SIZE	5 gallons (18.9 L)
ORIGINAL GRAVITY	1.031
FINAL GRAVITY	1.006
IBU	2
SRM	2
ABV	3.8%

MALTS AND ADJUNCTS

3.25 pounds (1.48 kg) German Pilsner Malt

1.85 pounds (0.84 kg) German Wheat Malt

3.5 ounces (100 g) Acidulated Malt

8.3 pounds (3.8 kg) Pitted and Lightly Stewed Greengage Plums (or similar)

HOPS (0-MINUTE BOIL)

1.75 ounces (50 g) Spalt (4% AA) Mash Hop

YEAST

1 package Fermentis SafAle US-05 Dry Yeast

1.5 L starter *Lactobacillus* *

1 package Wyeast 5112 *Brettanomyces* Bruxellensis

* "I'd like to keep semiquiet about my blend, but it does include Wyeast 5335. It's a great strain for gentle acidity and a fruity lacto funk when used in the primary ferment. Have fun finding the strain or blend of strains that provides the funk and acidity you prefer. Just don't kettle sour the beer."

NOTES

Mash Mash in temperature, 129°F (54°C), 15 minutes

Decoction Mash Pull ⅓ of mash and heat to conversion temperature 145°F (63°C), stirring constantly. Rest for 20 minutes and then bring to a boil. Return the decoction to the main mash, stopping at 145°F (63°C). Stir in mash hops. Rest for 45 minutes. Pull ⅓ of the mash and bring to the boil before returning it to main mash. Raise temperature to 154°F (68°C). Rest for 10 minutes and then sparge.

Brewing Heat the wort until almost boiling, then immediately chill to 64–68°F (18–20°C).

Fermenting Pitch both the ale yeast and *Lactobacillus*. Allow the fermentation to free rise above 68°F (20°C) ambient, reaching around 73°F (23°C). When primary fermentation nears completion, add the plums and *Brettanomyces*, taking care to avoid oxygen pickup. Age the beer for 14 weeks or until the terminal gravity is stable.

Post-fermentation Bottle condition, aiming for 3.7 volumes of CO_2.

4

THE CREATIVE FRONT

Rules? Who needs 'em. These forward-thinking, flavor-crazed homebrewers twist up new techniques and toss anything and everything into their brew kettles.

BEER WASN'T ALWAYS A FROTHING land of IPAs, imperial stouts, and fruited sours available at every supermarket and gas station. Light lagers, fizzy and see-through as a pint of seltzer, used to rule the landscape. Drinkers seeking fuller-flavored ales and lagers faced a conundrum: beer everywhere but nothing worth drinking.

Desire sparked creation. Homebrewers made what they couldn't find, loading fermenters with clones of Chimay Red, Dogfish Head 60 Minute IPA, Sierra Nevada Pale Ale, and Westmalle Tripel. But those same fires aren't burning as brightly anymore. Erstwhile rarities such as Stone IPA and Bell's Two Hearted Ale now line shelves in much of America. Why brew what you can buy?

Fewer homebrewers are grabbing their brew kettles to fill a flavor void. Instead, creativity compels them to deploy herbs, spices, fruits, and grains in new formulations. They're brewing what never existed before, harnessing their imaginations and global foodways to create the next must-drink beers. They're reconfiguring Hong Kong milk tea into a lightly tannic happy hour indulgence and creating lemongrass-laced ales perfect for brewing in Nevada's scorching Black Rock Desert. In Poland, brewers are using indigenous smoked plums and even herring, while their Berliner brethren are altering legendary beers such as Rodenbach and Orval with aftermarket additions of souring bacteria and berries.

Brewing's lack of rules, well, rules.

LUIS ARCE

○

TICOBIRRA
SAN JOSÉ, COSTA RICA
ticobirra.com

At a party in England, a friend offered computer engineer Luis Arce a beer that opened a door to a new world. The concept of homebrew had never crossed the Costa Rican's mind. "I never thought you could brew beer at home," says Arce, who had moved to Newcastle to work for Hewlett-Packard.

Arce was used to light lagers produced in huge factories by faceless people. Intrigued, he began homebrewing with his friend. But when his contract ended, so did his burgeoning hobby. Back in rainforest-covered Costa Rica, ingredients and equipment proved impossible to find.

Engineers live to solve problems, however. Arce ordered ingredients from America—a pricey proposition wrapped in red tape—but then Customs regularly halted his shipments. "Brewing ingredients are considered a food product, and there are lots of regulations." Another solution: what about a homebrew shop? After all, beer is Costa Rica's most consumed beverage.

He partnered with David Lockshin, a veteran beer distributor for Sierra Nevada and Sam Adams, to open TicoBirra, Costa Rica's first homebrew shop. It debuted on St. Patrick's Day, 2012, accompanied by a demo on brewing an Irish dry stout. "You can open a homebrew shop and stock the ingredients, but you need to teach and share your knowledge. The more we share, the better it is for the market," he says, adding that early classes were always free. "We decided to make the learning part easy for everyone."

FUN FACT

Many Costa Ricans brew Irish red ales because the country's first brewery, Costa Rica's Craft Brewing Company, started with a golden ale and an Irish red ale. "It was the very first craft beer for most Costa Ricans," says Arce.

TicoBirra (*tico* is slang for a Costa Rican) has become a one-stop shop for every budding beer geek. You can buy local beers alongside Chimay and Stone IPA, plus starter brewing kits, grains, and Pacific Northwest hops. "We are definitely very influenced by the U.S. Cascade is the best-selling hop."

When Arce began brewing, he liked making big, massively flavored beers. As an instructor, though, he preaches the beauty of starting simple and typically opens with a witbier. "You don't want to do something too crazy for the classes because people will get lost and frightened." But complexity comes in time. Former students have started influential Costa Rican breweries such as Treintaycinco, which makes piña colada–inspired pale ales and saisons studded with local

fruit. Arce sees room for growth for Costa Rican beer, especially on the supply side. "Even though we have improved with the variety of malt and yeast, we're still far from the variety in the U.S. Liquid yeast has been available only for a few months. That's difficult for homebrewers who like to replicate all that they see on the Internet."

Instead of imitating, Costa Rica offers a rich agricultural bounty—guava, mangos, soursop, tamarind—to create indigenous styles. "Some of the best-selling craft beers are fruitier styles," he says. Arce is always happy to offer guidance and answer any brewing queries about ingredients from dragon fruit to hops. "It's not just about opening a homebrew shop. It's also about creating a culture."

ADVICE

"We're a tropical country. I always tell people how important it is to keep beer under control during the first couple days of fermentation."

BREWER SPOTLIGHT

Homebrewer Alex Tweet was working in human resources when he took first place for the curry-laced stout that became Indra Kunindra. He later brewed for Ballast Point, developing Grapefruit Sculpin, before helping launch Modern Times and settling in at Fieldwork Brewing in Berkeley. Tweet makes some of the West Coast's top IPAs and intensely flavored beers, including Good Conduct. His bourbon barrel–aged, maple syrup–infused imperial brown ale—based on a homebrew recipe—won silver at the 2016 Great American Beer Festival.

DARTH WIT STOUT
Wheat Stout
LUIS ARCE

"I was a consumer of unflavored commercial beer until I moved to Newcastle, England, back in 2008. Stouts were my introduction to the real beer world, so it's a style I still enjoy a lot. Roasted wheat adds a twist to the traditional style. The stout has complex notes of coffee but less astringency, which helps with the drinkability."

SIZE	5 gallons (18.9 L)
ORIGINAL GRAVITY	1.060
FINAL GRAVITY	1.012
IBU	39
SRM	67
ABV	6.1%

MALTS AND ADJUNCTS

7.05 pounds (3.2 kg) Castle Château Pilsen Malt
0.88 pound (0.4 kg) Castle Château Wheat Blanc Malt
0.88 pound (0.4 kg) Castle Château Chocolat Malt
0.33 pound (0.15 kg) Castle Château Black Malt

HOPS (60-MINUTE BOIL)

0.8 ounce (23 g) Columbus (14% AA), 60 minutes
1 ounce (28 g) U.K. Fuggle (4% AA), 2 minutes

YEAST

1 package Fermentis SafAle S-33 Dry Yeast

NOTES

Mash Mash temperature, 52°F (67°C), 60 minutes
Mash out temperature, 158°F (70°C), 15 minutes

Brewing Cool wort to around 75°F (24°C).

Fermenting Ferment at 65°F (20°C).

ANNA BERKEN & CHARLIE SWEATT

LONG BEACH, CALIFORNIA

During college in Minnesota, Anna Berken dabbled in homebrewing with a crowd of bike-riding punks. She picked up the hobby, moved to Austin to work for a newspaper as a graphic designer, and met Charlie Sweatt. The twosome turned brewing into date night. "It was something that we could do as a new couple that was fun," Sweatt says.

They re-created favorite beers, including Real Ale's Firemans #4 Blonde Ale, and found their groove with saisons, witbiers, and the odd Belgian IPA. "Texas was so hot, and we didn't have sufficient temperature control for our beer," says Berken. "Saisons and Belgians always turned out well in the high temperatures."

After moving to Long Beach, California, they began attending Burning Man in 2012, bringing bottles of homebrew to share. Halfway through the week, communal goodwill turned to good grief: The bottles overheated and exploded. Weaponized shards of glass shredded everything. "After that, we realized kegs are the way to go," Berken says. The following year on the *playa*, they dragged out their brewing kit, started doing demonstrations, and got married. "In hindsight, it was ridiculous," says Sweatt. "But it started our tradition."

Controlling temperature and creating a contaminant-free fermentation require fastidious attention to detail. So imagine, then, that you decide to homebrew in one of America's most inhospitable environments: northwest Nevada's Black Rock Desert. A Bible's worth of plagues—gale-force winds, choking dust storms, triple-digit daytime temperatures, teeth-chattering cold at night—besets this tinder-dry expanse of alkaline flats ringed by barren mountains. The climate is fit for neither man, woman, nor yeast strain. But for one week in late August until Labor Day, Burning Man takes place here, the annual 70,000-person bacchanal of art, oddities, nudity, and, for Berken and Sweatt, plenty of beer and brewing.

For their first Burn brew, they added San Diego Super Yeast, a strain that ferments super-fast, and fermented in the keg. A steady stream of fellow burners relieved the pressure. "Every time we'd push the release valve, a spray of foam would come out of the top," Berken laughs. "We started getting a little worried."

They tapped the keg the last day of the festival. "It was like bread beer, like you were eating a meal," says Sweatt.

"We ended up drinking the whole keg before the burn," Berken adds. "It wasn't good, but we drank it."

One year, the couple and friends attempted an experiment: brew, ferment, and drink the beer in less than a week. So now, each August, the couple packs a vehicle with all the essentials needed to survive seven days in Black Rock City, the temporary enclave's nickname. Sunscreen, water, and shade structures accompany a jockey box, homebrew-filled kegs, and brewing equipment used for desert demos. "It really becomes performance art," Sweatt says. "It gives us an opportunity to explain the process, what beer is to us, and how fermentation works."

"It's great to see that realization go off in peoples' minds: *Wow, you can brew beer in one of the most inhospitable places?*" says Berken. "We're just out there with a burner, a propane tank, and a pot. People have no idea that there are organisms that turn sugar water into alcohol."

Berken and Sweatt belong to Orphan Endorphin, one of several organized camps that run pop-up homebrew pubs, and they help organize a Burning Man homebrew-pub crawl. Any Burner is welcome to sample the couple's kölsch, saisons, and witbiers that slice through the swelter. "I can't handle an IPA when it's 100 degrees outside," says Sweatt.

"We have a motto at our bar: Strange but tasty," adds Berken. "I like to engage with people and ask them what their tastes are. It makes them realize there are options other than Bud Light."

In line with Burning Man's barter-driven economy, customers pay nothing. "We always have so much beer that, for us, it's nothing to give our beer away," Sweatt says. Keeping it cold is tougher, though. At night, they store kegs outside to chill down, then bring them into the shade at daybreak when Orphans head to the ice distribution center to grab enough bags (trucked in daily) to fill the jockey box. Maintaining cold, stable temperatures is vital, as is steadily pouring pints; no beer grows warm and foamy in the tap lines.

"We call ourselves lazy brewers," says Berken. "We like to experiment with things, but we're not too particular about pH or temperature control. We just stick to recipes that we know will turn out OK." Don't mistake their self-professed laziness for carelessness, though. "We're really good at sanitization. We've never had anything we've had to pour down the drain because it got contaminated," Berken says.

They often brew at the festival's end, toting the wort back home to pitch yeast. (They do a partial mash to save water and cut down on soggy grains.) Back home in Long Beach, the couple's setup is essentially the same as in the desert: propane burner, beverage cooler, and a big ol' pot. "You really just need to start out with a good pot," Sweatt says. They offer proof positive that you don't need to spend thousands on shiny equipment, provided that you keep everything clean.

"If you put sugar water in a jug, as long as it's sanitized, it'll turn into something," Berken says. "It's hard to mess up."

ADVICE

Share your beer. "When you do five gallons at a time, sometimes you're sick of that recipe after drinking 50 beers of it. You start sharing it a lot more."

CAMPOUT LEMONGRASS ALE
Pale Ale
ANNA BERKEN & CHARLIE SWEATT

"This lemongrass ale is a refreshing, tangy brew made for hot days in the desert. The recipe is easy to make and serves as an introduction to the variety of ingredients you can use to make beer."

SIZE	5 gallons (18.9 L)
ORIGINAL GRAVITY	1.56
FINAL GRAVITY	1.14
IBU	21
SRM	4
ABV	6%

MALTS AND ADJUNCTS

2.5 pounds (1.13 kg) 2-Row Malt
5.5 pounds (2.49 kg) Pilsner Malt
8 ounces (0.23 g) Honey Malt
1 pound (0.45 kg) Honey

HOPS (60-MINUTE BOIL)

1 ounce (28 g) East Kent Golding (5% AA), 60 minutes
0.5 ounce (14 g) Saaz (3.75% AA), 15 minutes
4 ounces (113 g) Lemongrass (fresh)

YEAST

1 package Wyeast 1056 American Ale

NOTES

Mash Mash temperature, 155°F (68°C), 60 minutes
Sparge temperature, 170°F (77°C)

Brewing Add 1 pound honey with 60 minutes remaining in the boil. Add 4 ounces lemongrass with 10 minutes remaining in the boil. Cool wort to 80°F (27°C).

MARY IZETT & CHRIS CUZME

FIFTH HAMMER BREWING
BROOKLYN, NEW YORK
fifthhammerbrewing.com

f a beer-mad scientist created the ideal brewing couple, it would look like these two. Their Brooklyn loft apartment brims with air locks, clamps, cultures, hops, and hoses. Ferments such as Izett's honey-driven Elvis Sammy Short Mead (bacon, bananas, and peanut butter) or Cuzme's smoky pale ale gurgle happily.

Mary Izett moved to New York City in 2001 with her then-husband, drinking up the city's potential. "New York is too expensive not to take advantage of it," says Izett, who started leading beer tastings for friends. "They were like, 'It's obvious you need to start homebrewing.' So I did."

The pharmaceutical sales rep joined the Malted Barley Appreciation Society and New York City Homebrewers Guild (NYCHG), later becoming president of both. She also became a nationally ranked beer judge. At home, she focused on sours, Finnish sima, fast-fermenting ciders, and absinthe-inspired sodas. No experiment sounded too eccentric.

Chris Cuzme, a gregarious sax player, had moved to New York City to pursue a life in music. Low-paying gigs prompted him to take a rent-paying job at Merrill Lynch. Extra pocket cash became a homebrew kit, and down the rabbit hole he went. A molasses porter led to English browns and milds. Revelatory food pairings—witbier with a goat cheese and green apple omelet, for example— helped him turn his palate into a well-tuned instrument.

Nearly 9 million people live in the Sleepless City, but the homebrewing scene is a small world. Cuzme also joined the NYCHG, later becoming president as well, and met Izett, who ran a food and beer meet-up group. "Our love of pairing beer and food and sharing it with people brought us together," Cuzme says. The twosome launched a beer-pairing business that, like a slow ferment, steadily evolved. "We spent years as friends and business partners before becoming romantically involved."

The couple collaborated on a series of funky, smoky, tart Pillow Talk beers, including Sour Seduction, a Berliner weisse flavored with campfire-scented Lapsang Souchong tea. Customers bought their burgeoning romance by the pint. "There's a cool yin and yang to what we have together," Cuzme says. "Pillow Talk celebrates where Mary and I meet each other. We're both very different brewers."

Cuzme helped open Wandering Star Craft Brewery in Massachusetts before becoming head brewer at 508 GastroBrewery back in New York City. The licensed two-barrel basement brewery functioned as a glorified homebrew setup. He had creative carte blanche there and helped rebuild it after Hurricane Sandy submerged literally everything. He remained hyperaware of any microbe that could infect his beer, cleaning and sanitizing with religious zeal. "Sour beer was a bad word until I started brewing with Mary," he says. Izett's science background, on the other hand, prompted her to pack her basement with long-term sour projects. Contagion was the name of her game.

Her curiosity led her to fast fermentables such as short meads, flavoring them with blueberries and nutmeg, mangos and chiles, peaches and thyme. "I love taking inspiration from the seasons to ferment," says Izett, who tinkered with rhubarb soda, spearmint kombucha, and spinach wine. She turned her rapid-fire ferments into *Speed Brewing*, a guide for time-crunched brewers.

Cuzme's long-gestating project, Fifth Hammer Brewing, opened in Queens in 2017. After more than a decade yo-yoing between homebrewing and the professional circuit, Cuzme finally has a perch on which to play sax and brew what he pleases. "I can't live without feeding both sides of my creativity," he says. The brewery serves Cuzett Libations, releasing whatever ferment catches their fancy. "We called it Cuzett Libations and not Cuzett Brewing because we love cider, mead, and everything else," Izett says.

These days they also host the weekly *Fuhmentaboudit!* radio show, interviewing kimchi craftsmen and wild yeast–obsessed brewers, later bopping to breweries where Cuzme blows his saxophone and Izett leads workshops on, say, clothing repair.

"Neither of us is very good at sitting down and not doing anything," Cuzme says.

ADVICE

- "Don't be afraid, as long as you're cleaning, cleaning, cleaning and sanitizing, sanitizing, sanitizing."

- "Never assume your beer is bad. Taste it before you throw it out. There are certain flavors that you cannot fix, but through blending you can fix certain flavors. As a homebrewer, you can always change a beer. You're not beholden to a name. Change the beer into something that might work. Add some fruit, hit it with *Brettanomyces* or souring bacteria."

BREWER SPOTLIGHT

New York City homebrewer Rich Buceta left the advertising world to launch SingleCut Beersmiths, a brewery in Queens that specializes in whistle-clean pilsners, such as 19-33 and haze-crazed, hop-drenched Northeast-style IPAs, including the arrestingly tropical Softly Spoken Magic Spells Double IPA and the pine-and-pineappley Billy Half Stack IPA.

HOMEBREW WORLD

SZECHUAN PARADISE SAISON
CHRIS CUZME

"In winter 1999, a few years before my official leap into home zymurgy, I was hired to play jazz saxophone in Chengdu, the capital of China's Sichuan province. The club was a side project for the man who had founded three of Chengdu's best Sichuan restaurants and loved jazz. As his guests and seemingly the only Westerners in town, we dined in his establishments daily before gigs and ate every delicious thing brought to our table. My favorite dishes included Sichuan peppercorns, due to their zesty aromas and fascinating mouth-numbing tingle. This beer is my tribute. It has a zesty lemon character that dances and plays with the spicy intrigue of Sichuan peppercorns alongside the bitterness of grains of paradise."*

*"Szechuan" refers to the cuisine and therefore is how I spelled the beer name. The province and the peppercorns that grow there generally are spelled "Sichuan."

SIZE	5 gallons (18.9 L)
ORIGINAL GRAVITY	1.065
FINAL GRAVITY	1.006
IBU	25
SRM	4
ABV	7.7%

MALTS AND ADJUNCTS

9 pounds (4.1 kg) Belgian Pilsner Malt

2 pounds (0.9 kg) Wheat Malt

1 pound (0.45 kg) Candi Sugar

0.75 ounce (21 g) Lemon Peel

0.25 ounce (7 g) Grains of Paradise

0.25 ounce (7 g) Sichuan Peppercorns

HOPS (60-MINUTE BOIL)

2 ounces (56 g) Saaz (4% AA), 60 minutes

0.75 ounce (21 g) Saaz, Whirlpool

YEAST

2 packages Wyeast 3711 French Saison

NOTES

Mash Mash temperature, 149°F (66°C), 75 minutes

Sparge temperature, 168°F (75°C)

Brewing Add candi sugar for the last 15 minutes of the boil. Add lemon peel, grains of paradise, and peppercorns at the end of the boil.

Fermenting Begin fermentation at 65°F (18°C) and allow to free rise until fermentation completes, with a final gravity around 1.006.

Post-fermentation Bottle to 2.7 volumes CO_2.

PEOPLE'S PINT BREWING COMPANY

TORONTO, ONTARIO
peoplespint.com

Attend too many beer fests, and they'll bleed together like ink on a wet page: the same brewers, the same flagship IPAs, the same two-ounce serving glass. "There was nothing new, nothing exciting," Toronto homebrewer Doug Appeldoorn recalls of one tiresome gathering. *Wouldn't it be rad*, he thought, *to throw a party where homebrewers served their wildest and most wonderful small-batch marvels?*

That idea sprouted into the People's Pint event series, which starred the cream of Toronto's hoppy crop. Appeldoorn and partner Peter Caira, also a homebrewer, thoroughly vetted each beer's quality. Easy enough. The real challenge lay in obeying the law. "You can't serve homebrew and sell it," says Appeldoorn.

As a workaround, he created a homebrew appreciation club, offering free samples to members. "You just have people buy the glass, and the glass is $45." Those first sips of homemade beer challenged the long-held beliefs and opinions of numerous attendees. "Many people were thoroughly surprised at how good the homebrews were."

But you can doggy-paddle in legal gray areas for only so long. To rise aboveboard, Appeldoorn arranged for homebrewers to cart their equipment to breweries, where they brewed in licensed facilities. That arrangement culminated in an event for the 2016 Toronto Beer Week that featured 30 brewers. "It was like herding cats," Appeldoorn says of the challenge.

Putting the festivals out of their misery, he resurrected the concept as the brick-and-mortar People's Pint Brewing Company, where offerings cooked up by Toronto's top homebrewers complement house-made drafts. "If they want to brew a light lager, we're going to let them do it. It's basically whatever strikes their fancy."

Homebrewers receive enough ingredients to make a pilot beer. If it's successful, they receive an invitation to brew a larger batch on the brewery's system (repurposed soup kettles that used to make industrial stocks) and a stipend for their work. Appeldoorn sees the People's Pint as more than just another brewery, though; it's a community hub where homebrewers can use the quality assurance lab to ensure that each batch is better than the last. "Peter and I both started as homebrewers, and we want to continue to support and foster talented brewers in our city," he says.

JORDAN KOSTELAC

HONG KONG, CHINA

Moving to a foreign country means hankering for a taste of home: New York City–style pizza in Norway, Texas brisket in Turkey, or, for workplace strategist Jordan Kostelac, Bell's Oberon in Hong Kong.

"I can't tell you how many bottles of Oberon I drank in my life," Kostelac says. He grew up in Ohio, and his dad homebrewed for nearly three decades. Kostelac the younger was too young to participate, but the carboy never falls far from the family tree. When he moved to Hong Kong nearly a decade ago, he found an ocean of lagers as far as he could see.

"I wanted stuff I couldn't get here, so I started making it in my house," he says. "I was homebrewing out of necessity."

FUN FACT

In Hong Kong, locals colloquially call craft beer *gweilo leung cha*—essentially, the white ghost's herbal tea. *Gweilo* is Cantonese slang for a Westerner. "It's this idea that when the Chinese get sick, they drink herbal tea," Kostelac says. "When we get sick, we drink beer."

Kostelac bought a five-gallon starter kit, and "as soon as I got my hands on it I went crazy," he says. Forget San Diego IPAs; he spiced saisons with jasmine, made mulled wine–flavored beer, and mimicked the city's unofficial drink, black Ceylon tea mixed with condensed milk. "I'll give it to a local person and they'll say, 'You can do that with beer?' It makes craft beer more of a uniter than a divider."

Necessity often breeds ingenuity. Kostelac treats his adopted homeland as his homebrewing muse, adding anything and everything Hong Kong can offer to the brew kettle. Ever wonder what candied roast pork (*char siu*) would taste like in a porter? Well, Kostelac did. From his favorite store, he grabbed a big bowl of "fatty, sugary, amazingly savory" *char siu* sauce. "They thought I was crazy," he laughs. The saccharine sauce mostly fermented out of the beer. "It tasted like a perfectly passable porter, but it didn't taste like *char siu*."

He brews in his 300-square-foot apartment, battling Hong Kong's unwavering weather. "Hong Kongers will tell you Hong Kong has four seasons. That's not the case. It's hot, very hot, and sometimes less hot." He maintains fermentation temperatures with a wine fridge just big enough for five 1-gallon carboys, splitting the batches for experimentation.

Some succeed, some fail. Some failures also wind up succeeding. Take the time Kostelac brewed a blonde ale and added peeled lychees, forgetting to sanitize the fruit. "I didn't know what I didn't know," he says. Those lychees led to a *Lactobacillus* infection, which turned the blonde tart and tasty. "People just ate the sour up," he recalls. Mistakes can serve as learning opportunities. When

he was teaching a friend to brew, she wondered why he skipped sanitation. "I actually *want* something that seems bad to happen," he says. "That process of discovery is fun."

Kostelac harbors zero aspirations to brew beyond his apartment, and he gives away as much as he brews, clearing space to create his next curiosity. "I don't care about competition medals. I'm more excited to push the boundaries of what we can do with brewing and brewing techniques."

ADVICE

Always take notes, *especially* when you're just messing around. One brew day, Kostelac created a kitchen-sink batch of leftover liquid malt, added cherry and vanilla flavorings, and French-pressed the hops. The magnificent mutt wowed the judges in the homebrew competition he jokingly entered. "It was this great beer that I honestly can't reproduce because I forgot to take notes," he says. Lesson learned.

BREWER SPOTLIGHT

Former Goldman Sachs employee Rohit Dugar helped kick-start Hong Kong's beer scene with the opening of Young Master Ales in 2013. It celebrates local tastes in beers such as the Cha Chaan Teng Gose, which takes its saline edge from salted limes, and a spring saison flavored with chrysanthemum, osmanthus, and jasmine.

HONG KONG MILK TEA ALE
Specialty Ale
JORDAN KOSTELAC

"This was designed originally with a porter base partly because of the beer's many layers of euphemism. Hong Kong is a major port city, and the beer has an original gravity of 1.088 and an 8.8% ABV target because the number eight is very lucky in Chinese culture. What quickly became apparent is that the porter/stout roast and tea flavor are incredibly difficult to balance. I scaled back to a brown ale base and let the tea help give the beer a bit of a dark color so it's somewhere between the two styles."

SIZE	5 gallons (18.9 L)
ORIGINAL GRAVITY	1.088 (1.077 before lactose)
FINAL GRAVITY	1.010
IBU	20
SRM	23
ABV	8.8%

MALTS AND ADJUNCTS

9.6 pounds (4.35 kg) 2-Row Malt

1.92 pounds (0.87 kg) Maris Otter

0.95 pound (0.43 kg) Biscuit Malt

0.95 pound (0.43 kg) Flaked Oats

0.95 pound (0.43 kg) Caramel Malt (80L)

0.42 pound (0.19 kg) Roasted Barley

1.54 pounds (0.7 kg) Lactose

Pinch (0.25 g) Nutmeg

2 gallons (7.5 L) Black Tea

HOPS (60-MINUTE BOIL)

1 ounce (28 g) Fuggles (4% AA), 60 minutes

1 ounce (28 g) Fuggles, 30 minutes

YEAST

1 package White Labs WLP002 English Ale

NOTES

Mash Mash temperature, 150–152°F (66–67°C), 60–70 minutes

Brewing Add lactose with 15 minutes left in the boil. Add nutmeg with 5 minutes left in the boil. Collect wort until you have 4 or 5 gallons. Boil down during 60 minutes to 3 gallons of finished wort. After the boil, add the tea to top up to 5 gallons of finished beer.

For the tea, I use whole-leaf Ceylon black tea and follow the instructions on the label but cut about 20 percent of the brewing time off and steep at a precise 212°F (100°C). You want the tea taste with as few tannins as possible. I brew the tea the previous day in two 1-gallon carboys, then refrigerate them for 24 hours.

HONG KONG HOMEBREWERS ASSOCIATION

facebook.com/brewers.hk

Eight or nine years ago in Hong Kong, Joshua Wolper went out with friends for drinks. One friend mentioned how much he missed fermenting his own alcohol. Wolper, a native Hong Konger who had spent time in New York and San Francisco, had no idea what his friend meant. "He was like, 'Oh man, fermentation is pretty easy,' " recalls Wolper, who went home with instructions to make hard cider (baker's yeast + pasteurized apple juice). Wolper wondered why it took so long to hear about home ferments. "Then I realized, *How come there's no active brewing culture in Hong Kong?*"

He filled that space by founding the Hong Kong Homebrewers Association and creating a monthly event for Hong Kongers to congregate, commiserate, and educate about brewing. Wolper has overseen the club's swelling ranks of natives and expats alike, measuring its growth by the number of entries in the annual competition. "A few years ago it was 20 entries, then it became 50 entries, and then 80 entries, and 150 entries." Winners collaborate with a local brewery, and Wolper continues exploring the fringes of fermentation. He makes mulberry mead with hand-harvested fruit and local honey and boosts cider's ABV with coconut sugar. "Orthodoxy is important, but once you know the rules you can break them."

CRISTAL PECK

SUNSHINE BREWERY / PARASITE PRODUKTIONS
BERLIN, GERMANY
facebook.com/parasiteproduktions

Raised in Australia, Cristal Peck had been around beer since she was young, watching her dad homebrew. "It was ingrained in me that I would eventually try it," she says. "My dad trained me to be a fan of beer. Having three daughters, he thought it was more parentally responsible of him to get us on beer instead of spirits."

She trained as a microbiologist, toiling in a lab before instructing high school students about, say, the enzymatic process or long sugars breaking down. "I was basically teaching kids to brew beer without using beer as the reference," she says.

Her brother bought her a starter kit, which proved exciting and irritating in equal parts. "I did one extract kit and straightaway lost patience," says Peck, who sought out Grape & Grain, a great Melbourne homebrew store, and jumped into all-grain brewing.

Come weekends in the Sunshine suburb of Melbourne, Peck unwound in her garden, tending to a vegetable patch, kicking back with her dog and ducks, and making beer in a shed under the name Sunshine Brewery. She brewed on a gravity-fed system fashioned from stainless-steel kegs and fed the spent grains to her ducks. The setup was idyllic, but wanderlust beckoned. She wanted to live in Europe and settled on Berlin, shuttling her brewing system into her dad's garage. "It was heartbreaking," she says.

Peck resumed brewing on a more rudimentary system in Germany. "I had to use my stovetop and do smaller batches. I didn't have a refrigerator with a thermostat. I lost total control." She soon landed a job in a science lab, injecting DNA into fruit fly embryos, and quickly found her homebrew footing as well. Her raspberry-infused Framboise Fantastic took top honors at the 2015 Berlin Beer Week, the recipe brewed professionally and distributed citywide.

Peck began managing Bierlieb, a homebrew shop and beer store, and taught classes that blended beer and science, uniting her two passions. She created new recipes, including a stout made with vegemite, and began brewing commercially with her boyfriend, Richie Hodges, the brewmaster at Berliner Berg. When Bierlieb closed in 2017, they plotted Parasite Produktions.

Orval, Rodenbach Grand Cru, and St. Bernardus Abt 12 are fabled and flawless. Why mess with perfection? Because they can. Peck and Hodges love adulterating revered beers. They dose the rich and malty Andechs Doppelbock Dunkel with souring bacteria and age the amalgam in wood. They add wild blueberries to Rodenbach's archetypal sour. Playful contamination distinguishes the efforts of Parasite Produktions.

"We've taken some of our favorite beers and meddled with them in a way that a good parasite does," says Peck.

In addition to doctoring beers, she and Hodges are thinking of creating a business that will allow them to gypsy-brew legally. "There are so many big breweries that are closing down," she says. "There's a culture of gypsy brewing in Germany, where breweries are encouraging people to come in. Like a good parasite, you have to exploit a situation," Peck smiles.

ADVICE

"Brew an infected batch once so you can see the importance of sanitization."

BREWER SPOTLIGHT

A chance meeting at an Illinois liquor store led homebrewers Marika Josephson, Aaron Kleidon, and Ryan Tockstein to launch Scratch Brewing Company. The farmhouse brewery focuses on beers made from foraged hickory bark, dandelions, pine needles, and homegrown turmeric. Check out their *Homebrewer's Almanac* to learn more about forage brewing.

FRAMBOISE FANTASTIC
Fruit Beer
CRISTAL PECK

"I love brewing with fruit. This tart and subtle framboise was the first I ever tried, and since then there's been no stopping me! I often use raspberries, but I also brew with rhubarb, peaches, and clementines. This beer evokes a juicy and plump berry harvest in drinkable form. At a delicate 5.5% ABV, Framboise Fantastic seeks to arouse the nuances of sweet and slightly tart raspberries, making it a refreshing and delicately hopped light autumn ale."

SIZE	5.28 gallons (20 L)
ORIGINAL GRAVITY	1.048
FINAL GRAVITY	1.003
IBU	20
SRM	7
ABV	5.5%

MALTS AND ADJUNCTS

1.76 pounds (0.8 kg) Weyermann Münchner Malt II
1.76 pounds (0.8 kg) Weyermann Pale Wheat Malt
4.85 pounds (2.2 kg) Weyermann Pale Ale Malt
0.44 pound (0.2 kg) Weyermann Acidulated Malt
2.87 pounds (1.3 kg) Fresh Raspberries (mashed)

HOPS (70-MINUTE BOIL)

0.8 ounce (23 g) Perle (7.6% AA), 60 minutes
1.75 ounces (50 g) Crystal (3.8% AA), Whirlpool

YEAST

1 package Danstar Belle Saison Dry Yeast

NOTES

Mash Mash in temperature, 140°F (60°C)

Mash temperature, 151°F (66°C), 60 minutes

Mash step temperature, 162°F (72°C), 20 minutes

Mash out temperature, 172°F (78°C), 5 minutes

Fermenting Once the beer has reached a gravity of 1.006, rack to sanitized carboy with raspberries. Resume the fermentation at 64-77°F (18–25°C) for 1 week or until the final gravity reaches 1.003.

Post-fermentation Keg or bottle at 2.5 volumes of CO_2.

FACTOTUM BREWHOUSE

DENVER, COLORADO
factotumbrewhouse.com

At a family dinner in the early 2010s, talk turned to Denver's booming homebrewing scene. *Why,* siblings Christopher and Laura Bruns wondered, *had no one tapped the city's homebrew talent and served it in a taproom?* Several years passed, and nothing changed. "We said, 'Well, if no one else is going to do it, we should,' " recalls Christopher.

The duo enrolled in brewing and business classes, then Frankensteined a brewhouse with old dairy and wine equipment. The concept launched in spring 2015 and quickly took off. "Since we've opened, we've consistently had a yearlong queue. We've had a few brewers who, as soon as they brew, get right back in line," Laura says. "I feel bad when I tell people, 'Hey, you've got at least a year before you can brew.' "

Laura initially thought customers would boil up a bunch of IPAs at Factotum. Not so. "Most people want to brew some of the weirdest, craziest stuff," she says. "It's their one chance, and they're like, 'I'm not going to blow it on a West Coast IPA. That's too normal.' "

The beers are as devil-may-care as anything you can dream up. Perhaps an IPA laced with lavender and white tea will win over your heart. Maybe you want that milk stout made with cacao nibs and roasted peanuts followed by a porter mobbed with molasses and maple syrup. Factotum welcomes beer enthusiasts and amateur brewers to create a recipe or flavor profile, then collaborate with head brewer Christopher to fashion a batch later served in the taproom. Guest brewers pay for the privilege but receive plenty of beer and perks in the form of consumer feedback and no janitorial duties.

"I tell people, 'Part of the fee is that you don't have to clean up,' " says Christopher. "But some people want the full experience and clean up anyway."

Some customers love the endless variety, while others just want to grab that stout they tried last week. Revolving trials such as Sublimation, a cherry tea–flavored tripel, stoke interest and ire in equal measure. To split the difference, Christopher honed an always-on-tap pilsner enriched with a small charge of melanoidin malt. "We have 14 taps. It's OK to have some fun stuff on, but you need some standbys as well."

Few brewing at Factotum harbor next-step fantasies. "Most do it for fun," Christopher says, which makes the brewery a net win for all. Amateurs sample the professional life, and Christopher constantly hones his skills. "Everyone comes in with a new idea, and I need to make it work. It's made me a better brewer."

FUN FACT

Each year at the Great American Beer Festival's Pro-Am Competition, amateurs team up with professional brewers to create incredibly forward-thinking beers, such as Just Another Pretty Face, a whiskey barrel–aged barley wine collab between Denver Beer Company and Doug Thiel that won in 2017.

PLIMMÓ

Even rock-solid friendships can fracture. As the years disappear, careers, marriages, and kids consume ever-larger chunks of time, meaning fewer hours for crushing beers with buds.

"We needed to find a common hobby that would force us to get together," anthropologist Pétur Waldorff says of his group of six friends. It was 2009, a sad moment for flavor and selection in Iceland.

"At that time, you could basically get only yellow lager," says Halldór Halldórsson, a brand manager for Stella Artois.

Nearly 200 batches later, Plimmó (a nonsensical word that the friends made up nearly two decades ago for a drinking game), the sextet's homebrew collective, has become one of Iceland's most imaginative and resourceful. They brew IPAs, amber ales, and imperial stouts alike in a repurposed midcentury washing machine. "People come to where we brew and laugh at our equipment because it's so old," says Waldorff, who first encountered homebrewing while living in Montreal.

Quality has increased greatly from their inaugural batches. Like many, the friends began with prehopped liquid extract. The results were appalling rather than appealing. By their fifth or sixth batch, they talked a local pro into providing ingredients—a stopgap at best. No Icelandic homebrew shops existed then, so Plimmó created its own supply chain. In 2010, they traveled to Belgium's Castle Malting and received the royal treatment. "We didn't say we had a brewery, but we said we were brewers," says Halldórsson. Plimmó signed a deal to import malted barley, hops, and yeast and sold raw materials to fellow brewers. "It wasn't about making money but spreading homebrewing, making it easier for people to get ingredients," Halldórsson says. (An Icelandic homebrew shop has opened since then, and Plimmó exited the distribution game.)

The friends meet regularly in their industrial space with the faintest inkling of what to make. "Someone starts milling the pale ale malt, and Pétur and I are working on the computer like, 'OK, let's do this, this, and this,'" says Halldórsson. "When someone gets an idea, we try to work with it."

Plimmó plays it fast, loose, and fun. For example, they forgo temperature control. "We like an X factor," Halldórsson says. "We don't want to overcontrol it and buy a contraption where we insert the ingredients and press play." The friends rarely repeat recipes and eagerly tackle experiments such as a strong Scotch ale boiled with hot stones—no electricity needed. "We went to a tombstone manufacturer and asked for leftovers," says Halldórsson. "I looked at some broken tombstones that said, like, 'Here lies blah blah blah.' I was like, 'Should we take this?' He said, 'No, no, I'm repairing that one.' We got some other granite and heated it on the barbecue. It was beer 37, and it was actually quite good."

Plimmó also made Iceland's first indigenous beer.

They bought barley from a farmer in southern Iceland, then malted and dried the grain. Hops grew wild in a member's backyard. They harvested some in August and dried them the next day. "We made the worst beer in the history of Iceland," Halldórsson says. "We got a really bad transformation of the starches. It was like drinking yellow mud."

Their creativity didn't end there, though. Plimmó has made hazy New England IPAs and imperial IPAs with ABVs creeping illicitly toward double digits. That's right: In Iceland, it's still against the law to homebrew beer stronger than 2.25 percent, a lingering hangover from nearly 75 years of Prohibition. "It's illegal but not really enforced," Waldorff says, noting that the club taught an introductory homebrew class to employees of Vínbúð, the state-run chain of alcohol and tobacco stores. "At first we thought it was a setup, but they were so interested and so happy to hear from us."

FUN FACT

March 1, known as Beer Day, commemorates the end of Prohibition in Iceland. The booze ban started in 1915, underwent modification in 1935 that permitted beer up to 2.25% ABV, and finally ended altogether in 1989.

Plimmó has no plans to go pro. The pals are content to pour beer at local festivals, brew for competitions, and keep their friendship flowing, one communal pint after another.

ADVICE

"Don't invest too heavily in equipment," says Halldórsson, who found Plimmó's washing-machine brew kettle abandoned outside an apartment building. "Have patience and wait for the equipment to find you. It's much more fun to build a brewery your own way. If you maintain it well, you'll like the brewery more than if you take the equipment out of a box that cost you $2,000."

BREWER SPOTLIGHT

Brugghús Steðja harnesses Iceland's terroir in Hvalur 2, a seasonal ale made with sheep dung–smoked whale testicles. You'd be nuts not to try it once.

OOMPA LOOMPA IMPERIAL STOUT
PLIMMÓ

This warming imperial stout is strong enough to ward off any wintry chill, in Iceland and elsewhere. Like Plimmó, make sure you share the beer with your very best friends.

SIZE	5 gallons (18.9 L)
ORIGINAL GRAVITY	1.095
FINAL GRAVITY	1.021
IBU	77
SRM	43
ABV	9.9%

MALTS AND ADJUNCTS
13.9 pounds (6.3 kg) Pale Ale Malt (3°L)
1.3 pounds (0.6 kg) Munich Malt (6°L)
1.1 pounds (0.5 kg) Roasted Barley (400°L)
0.95 pound (0.43 kg) Weyermann Carafa I
10 ounces (0.29 kg) Weyermann CaraMunich I
10 ounces (0.29 kg) Briess Carapils
1.8 ounces (50 g) Flaked Wheat
1 ounce (28 g) Flaked Barley

HOPS (60-MINUTE BOIL)
1 ounce (28 g) East Kent Golding (5% AA), 60 minutes
2.4 ounces (68 g) Fuggles (4% AA), 60 minutes
0.5 ounce (14 g) Columbus (15% AA), 60 minutes
0.5 ounce (14 g) Styrian Golding (3% AA), 60 minutes
1 ounce (28 g) East Kent Golding, 10 minutes
1.3 ounces (37 g) Fuggles, 10 minutes

YEAST
3 packages Wyeast 1056 American Ale

NOTES
Mash Mash temperature, 151°F (66°C), 75 minutes
Mash out temperature, 168°F (75.6°C), 15 minutes

Brewing Cool wort to around 70°F (21°C).

Fermenting Ferment at 68°F (20°C) for 17 days. Move to a secondary fermenter and keep at 57°F (14°C) for 2 weeks.

Post-fermentation To boost aroma and flavor, add vanilla beans from ½ vanilla pod sterilized for 24 hours with a dash of bourbon. Cold crash at 32–39°F (0–4°C) for 1 week.

WICHIT SAIKLAO

BANGKOK, THAILAND

facebook.com/chitbeer

The fighting spirit took root in Wichit "Chit" Saiklao at 17 years old when he received a military scholarship to study abroad. He chose the Virginia Military Institute and later attended Georgia Tech for his PhD in electrical engineering—and an introduction to homebrewing. On weekends, he hung out with a friend and sampled his homebrew. The taste impressed him less than the possibility. *One day I'm going to brew*, thought Chit, who imagined he'd be 55 or 60 by then and the hobby would carry him into old age. Chit forgot about this promise to himself and returned to Thailand in 2003.

Then, one fateful night in his forties he found himself at a Bangkok bar. The beer list stretched 100 deep, and hundreds of empties doubled as decoration. "I kept asking, 'What's going on? Where have I been?'" he recalls.

Back home, he went online and bought a Mr. Beer kit from Amazon. The first batch failed, flat and sweet, as did the second. Maybe he wasn't cut out to be a brewer. A year later, he bought his home on Ko Kret, a small island where cars are banned and coconut and bananas trees grow tall and lush. At a friend's urging, he brewed one last batch in Mr. Beer.

"I read the menu, line by line, one more time, and the last line said, 'Sprinkle the yeast under the lid,'" Chit recalls. *Wait, yeast?*

He thought the small packets were silica gel and had been throwing them away. He pitched the yeast, bubbles bubbled, and success. He invited friends over for a taste. "'Chit, am I sitting in Bavarian fields somewhere in Germany?'" he recalls a friend saying.

He started brewing all-grain by his thirteenth batch, importing ingredients from an Idaho brew shop, the only one that shipped to Thailand then. (Sourcing malts and hops is easier now, though fresh liquid yeast remains elusive.) Word of his beer spread online, and he freely poured pints for anyone who came to his home. Gifts beget a business, and in time he found himself operating an island brewery.

Thailand's rigid 1950 Liquors Act forbids homebrewing, though, and that includes owning any equipment. Break the law, and you'll risk fines and even

CHIT BEER
1
2 GoodChit Pilsner 4.9
3
4
5
6
7
8 Nut Brown
9
10
11
12
13
14 Bottle
PAIRING
DINNER NIGHT

jail time, especially if, for example, you open an illicit brewery and bar on an island 12 miles north of Bangkok. "I sell my beer. I've been caught three times already."

NOT SO FUN FACT ————————————

The maximum penalty for homebrewing in Thailand is six months in jail and a fine of 5,000 baht (approximately $150).

————————————————

Fines won't stop this Thai army colonel and homebrew revolutionary, though. Here in paradise he operates Chit Beer, an open-air compound consisting of a brewery and bar. Slogan: "Oh, it's good chit." His customers sip lemongrass kölsch and chrysanthemum pale ale while watching boats glide down the Chao Phraya River. More than 1,000 students have graduated from his homebrewing boot camp, and scores of them have launched their own underground brands.

"The way to liberate homebrewing is to create an army of brewers," says Chit. "A brewer is the ambassador of craft beer. Once they go out and they brew a good beer, the word spreads out wider and wider. In 2020 things are going to change." That's his target year for legalizing homebrew in Thailand, where 60 million people make do with just two lagers: Singha and Chang. "When I looked around Thailand, I saw a lot of beer monopolies. I feel that something was wrong in the industry, and I would like to change it."

Chit is pursuing that mission with Brewhouse of Friendship, an open-source brewpub where brewers can do R&D batches. He envisions a future with five or six open-source operations scattered across Thailand offering havens for homebrewers to brew up a national identity. "My hobby has a higher purpose to change something and spread good things," he says.

Running one multifaceted business would prove daunting for many people, but Chit also teaches electrical engineering at a military academy, oversees a couple of IT companies that he founded, and he opened Turtle Bar, which specializes in craft beer from Thailand and around the world. With each project, he gathers more energy and inspiration. "It's about correcting something that's been wrong in Thailand for a very long time," he says.

ADVICE

"Just brew. Once you've got your first sips of the beer, you can keep brewing and keep improving. Make the first batch as easy as possible. Once they brew the beer, people feel empowered like they can do something for themselves. That will make everything different."

BREWER SPOTLIGHT

Chicago-area homebrewer BJ Pichman now helms Forbidden Root, which makes botanically driven beers flavored with cardamom, licorice root, sandalwood, and more. His Fernetic recasts Fernet-Branca liqueur as a beguilingly aromatic beer.

CHRYSANTHEMUM TEA KÖLSCH
WICHIT SAIKLAO

"Chrysanthemum Flower Tea Kölsch is one of Chit Beer's most popular beers. It might be because of its light and crispy character that fits perfectly with the hot weather in Thailand."

SIZE	5.28 gallons (20 L)
ORIGINAL GRAVITY	1.048
FINAL GRAVITY	1.012
IBU	23
SRM	2.9
ABV	4.7%

MALTS AND ADJUNCTS

7 pounds (3.18 kg) Pilsner Malt
1.5 pounds (0.68 kg) Vienna Malt
12 ounces (0.34 kg) Wheat Malt
1 pound (0.45 kg) Chrysanthemum Flower Tea

HOPS (60-MINUTE BOIL)

0.75 ounce (21 g) Hallertau Mittelfrueh (6% AA), 60 minutes
0.5 ounce (14 g) Saaz (4% AA), 20 minutes
0.5 ounce (14 g) Saaz, 5 minutes

YEAST

1 package Fermentis SafLager S-23 Dry Yeast

NOTES

Mash Mash temperature, 150°F (66°C), 60 minutes

Brewing Add 1 Whirlfloc tablet at 15 minutes remaining in the boil. Add chrysanthemum flower tea at 5 minutes remaining in the boil. Cool wort to less than 75°F (24°C).

Fermenting Ferment at 60°F (16°C) for 7 days. Transfer to a secondary fermenter and condition for an additional 7 to 14 days.

HOW TO LEAD A HOMEBREW TOUR

I stumbled into my tour guide role by following my gut, which often led me astray—like the time the subway train pulled away, leaving half of my group still on the platform. Through trial and error, I devised a pretty much foolproof formula for setting up homebrew tours. They're a fantastic way to showcase your city's amateur brewing scene as well as an opportunity for brewers to receive unvarnished, unfiltered feedback from total strangers. Here's how to set up your own homebrew tour.

Location, Location

Select brewers in a tight geographic area, which will reduce transit time. Walking is the ideal mode of transportation, followed closely by mass transit. A private tour bus is a great option in more suburban, spread-out towns, but cost can prove prohibitive. Bicycles, as mentioned on page viii, are a bad idea. *Always* include the full postal address, lest someone end up in the wrong borough or city.

The Magic Number

Order the tour by increasing talent: someone just starting out, an intermediate homebrewer, then an experienced amateur angling to go pro. Three is the magic number. However you stack it, aim to visit the most seasoned brewer last. Reach out to potential brewers six to eight weeks before the proposed date to give them plenty of time to cook up another batch if needed. Homebrew clubs are great resources for finding hosts.

Four!

Hours, that is. Keep each visit to between 45 minutes and an hour, which will make each stop feel like a pop-up party. Drinkers arrive in a thirsty stampede and leave before they overstay their welcome.

Tickets, Please

Online ticketing systems are easy to set up. I like Brown Paper Tickets (brownpapertickets.com). Since you're visiting private homes, it's respectful not to broadcast addresses. Instead, the ticket purchase triggers an email that features the gathering point. This is a good place to note that *all* attendees must meet the minimum legal drinking age in your country.

Pick a Number

Limit the number of attendees to 20 or 25. Ever tried to herd drunk cats?

Marching Orders

One week before the tour, send a reminder email with pertinent information, including the following: date, time, location, contact information, weather forecast, and what to bring (water, snacks, coat, umbrella, comfortable shoes, etc.).

Pour Move

People are happy to listen to pretty much anything if holding a cold one. Have the hosts pour attendees a beer upon arrival before their opening remarks.

Glass Act

Glasses are great, but doing dishes isn't. Plastic cups are perfect. The liquid inside matters most.

Say What

For opening remarks, ask the brewers to describe how they started, the styles that get them stoked and why, and what's on the menu. Five minutes is just right.

Word Up

No host should hold guests hostage like a boorish, rambling college professor. Let people talk among themselves and ask the brewer questions one on one. Some people will want to know about the brewing nitty-gritty, while others just want another pour of that pale ale.

The Spice of Life

Each brewer should pour at least two different beers, preferably three—or more if possible. Attendees would rather try sips of lots of different beers than glug a whole pint of just one. Plan for two or three ounces per sample.

Rule Number 1

Ten minutes before departing a stop, remind people to go to the bathroom. A full bladder waits for no one.

Clean Slate

At the end of each stop, ask the crowd to give a round of applause for the brewer and then have them toss their cups in the trash or recycling bin or bring their glasses to the sink. Act like the world's greatest houseguests.

Paying the Piper

Paying for homebrew is illegal, but giving it away in your home is totally aboveboard. (Note: Laws differ from country to country.) Consider compensating brewers with gift certificates to the local homebrew shop.

HOMEBREW COMPETITIONS

Quality doesn't divide amateur beer from professional. I've sent plenty of store-bought suds down the drain, and countless homebrews have made my taste buds somersault with joy. No, the line is a license, which fills the government's coffers with tax funds. More and more breweries are blurring that line by running homebrew competitions that reward amateurs with professionally brewed batches. Here are some of America's top homebrew contests. For a current list of competitions, visit the American Homebrewers Association website, homebrewersassociation.org.

Bell's Brewery Annual Homebrew Competition

Honoring the brewery's homebrew shop roots, this contest rewards the champ with a professionally brewed batch served at Bell's Eccentric Café in Kalamazoo, Michigan.

bellsbeer.com

The Bruery, Batch

This competition commemorates milestone brews (50, 300, 1,000, etc.) by packaging the winning recipe.

thebruery.com/events/homebrew

Fair State Brewing Cooperative Homebrew Member Challenge

Members of the Minneapolis coop brewery compete for a chance to have a 15-barrel version of their recipe brewed.

fairstate.coop

Make the Cut

Vermont's 14th Star Brewing Co. brews, cans, and distros this contest's top batch.

makethecut.beer

Reuben's Brews Hop Idol

Excel at IPAs? The Seattle brewery's competition rewards the finest hop-forward beers by brewing the winning batch on its system.

reubensbrews.com

Rhinegeist Homebrew Competition

The Cincinnati brewery packages the winning beer and distributes it in 22-ounce bottles and on draft.

rhinegeist.com/homebrew-competition

Sam Adams LongShot American Homebrew Competition

More than 1,000 people enter the contest annually, and the company packages the winning entry in six-packs and sells it nationwide.

samueladams.com/longshot

Stone American Homebrew Association Rally and Competition

The winners partner with a guest brewery to create a three-way collaboration that Stone then distributes nationwide.

stonebrewing.com

GLOSSARY OF SELECT TERMS

Adjunct Fermentable substances substituted for cereal grains, chiefly barley. Rice and corn can lighten a beer's body. (That's why Coors Light has an SRM of 1 or 2.) *Adjunct* may seem like an evil word, but, deployed judiciously, adjuncts can create delicious beer.

Alcohol This fermentation by-product occurs when yeast devours sugar in the wort. You can measure it in two ways, alcohol by volume (ABV) and alcohol by weight (ABW). In craft brewing, ABV is the standard measurement. Alcohol weighs about 80 percent as much as water, so to convert ABW to ABV, multiply by 1.25. (4.8% ABW = 6% ABV.)

Ale One of two big families of beer, the other being lager. Like your great aunt in Florida, ale yeasts favor warmer temperatures, hanging out at the top of the fermentation tank. Ale flavors and aromas are typically estery, or fruity, and can taste sweeter and more full-bodied than lagers. Ales encompass an enormous grab bag of styles, including Belgian strong ales and IPAs.

Alpha acids Found in the hop cone, these contribute bitterness to beer. They're water-insoluble naturally, but boiling them causes isomerization, which allows them to dissolve in water.

Aroma hops Hops used later in the boil for bouquet instead of bitterness.

Astringent A drying, puckering taste that's good or bad, depending on your taste buds.

Barley The main cereal grain used to make beer. After water, it's the biggest ingredient.

Barrel The standard measure for brewing. 1 barrel = 31 gallons (117.3 L). A keg is half a barrel.

Beta acids Also found in the hop cone, they primarily contribute to a beer's bouquet.

Bittering hops Used early in the boil to add bitterness instead of aroma.

Boil The stage at which the wort boils to kill bacteria and yeast and cause proteins to coagulate. Hops are added during this stage.

Bottle-conditioned Beer carbonated naturally by live yeast in the bottle.

Brew kettle The vessel in which the wort boils with hops.

Carboy Plastic or glass vessel used to ferment beer.

Cask A wooden, metal, or plastic vessel used to mature, ferment, or flavor beer.

Cicerone A beer sommelier who passes the Cicerone Certification Program.

Cornelius keg A stainless-steel container originally used by the soda industry to distribute concentrated syrup. Today, the corny, as it's known, is the homebrewer's favored container for kegging beer.

Double IPA A stronger, more intense IPA typically with a floor of 8% ABV. See *imperial IPA*.

Dry hopping Adding hops to beer that has finished fermenting or is conditioning. This step creates intense, fragrant, aromatic brews.

Fermentation The metabolic process by which yeast consumes sugar, creating alcohol and carbon dioxide.

Filtration The removal of any floating proteins and yeasts that creates a clearer, more stable—and sometimes less flavorful—beer.

The Secret Life of BEER!

BEER

Classic Bottled Beers of the World — ROGER PROTZ

Beer

Man Walks into a Pub — PETE BROWN

RED, WHITE, AND BREW — BRIAN YAEGER

Bernstein — BREWED AWAKENING

ALAN D. BUTCHER — Ale & Beer

JEREMY COWAN — CRAFT BEER Bar Mitzvah

MICHAEL JACKSON'S GREAT BEERS OF BELGIUM

MICHAEL JACKSON'S GREAT BEERS OF BELGIUM

Bernstein — BREWED AWAKENING

BARON — Brewed in America

Beer Encyclopaedia

STEVE HINDY — Beer Lover's New York

The Craft Beer Revolution

BEAUMONT — Beer for Pete's Sake

STEPHEN BEAUMONT — A Taste for Beer

Michael Jackson's Beer Companion — Premium Beer Drinker's Guide

The Taste of Beer — ROGER PROTZ

ULTIMATE

BEER

THE WORLD ATLAS OF BEER — Michael Jackson

Farmhouse Ales

NOONAN — New Brewing Lager Beer

brewing with WHEAT

THE HOME BREWER'S GUIDE TO VINTAGE BEER

Daniels & Larson — Smoked Beers

Daniels & Parker — Brown Ale

Classic Stout & Porter

h ps m lt y ast

BREW CHEMA 101

Final gravity (FG) A measure of the unfermentable substances remaining in beer after fermentation has finished. The lower the number, the drier the beer.

Flameout The moment that wort leaves the heat source. Hops added at this time impart more aroma and flavor. Also called *knockout*.

Fresh-hop beer A fragrant beer made with the year's first batches of dried hops. See *wet-hop beer*.

Hopback A sealed, hops-stuffed vessel, between brew kettle and wort chiller, through which the wort circulates, snatching up heady aromas and flavors. Also called a *hop jack*.

Hop bursting Adding massive amounts of hops during the end of the brewing process, drawing out intense flavors and aromas but little bitterness.

Hops The creeping bine (not vine) *Humulus lupulus*, which hails from the same family as cannabis. The female flowers, called *cones*, flavor beer and provide bitterness. Each variety has its own aroma or flavor profile. See *alpha acids* and *beta acids*.

Imperial IPA A stronger, more intense IPA. The phrase often is used interchangeably with *double IPA*, but the ABV may reach double digits, putting it closer to triple IPA territory.

India pale ale (IPA) A British-born, hop-focused style of beer that has become increasingly popular worldwide.

International bitterness unit (IBU) A scientific measure of bitterness. Low IBU (Budweiser registers around 11) means the beer isn't hoppy. In triple digits, you're in for a mouth-scrunching ride. It's not a perfect measure of perceived bitterness, though. A 5% ABV IPA with 50 IBUs will taste more intense than a 10% ABV IPA with 50 IBUs.

Knockout See *flameout*.

Krausen The foamy head, largely composed of yeast and wort proteins, that forms atop beer during fermentation.

Lager The other main style of beer. Like penguins, bottom-fermenting lager yeasts prefer cooler temperatures. They also take longer to ferment. (*Lagern* means "to rest" in German.) Lagers typically taste crisp, delicate, and as refreshing as a quick plunge in a cool lake in hot weather.

Malt Bathing cereal grains in water jump-starts germination, allowing the grain to create the enzymes required to convert starches and proteins into fermentable sugars. Heating and drying the grain halts the process. Like coffee, grain can be roasted to create different flavors and intensities.

Mash The initial step in brewing, in which crushed grain steeps in boiling water, transforming starches into sugars.

Mash tun The vessel in which mash boils.

Mouthfeel How beer subjectively feels when you drink it—a combination of body, texture, carbonation, and flavor.

Noble hops These aromatic, less bitter, European hop varieties, including Hallertauer, Saaz, Spalt, and Tettnanger, impart a spicy, herbal, zesty character. Commonly found in pilsners and European lagers.

Original gravity (OG) A measure of the fermentable sugars in wort, prior to pitching yeast. The higher the number, the more sugars are available to convert into alcohol.

Oxidation When oxygen hits beer, the liquid undergoes a series of chemical reactions that create stale flavors sometimes described as "sherry" or "cardboard."

Pasteurization Killing yeast by applying heat. Unpasteurized beers retain their yeast, which means the beer continues to evolve over time.

Pitch Adding yeast to cooled wort.

Priming Dosing a fermented beer in bottle or keg with priming sugar, which creates additional carbonation or flavors.

Rye A cereal grain that imparts spiciness and crispness, which help dry out beer.

Session beer Low in alcohol, not in flavor, ideal for sipping during long drinking sessions.

Skunked When UV light strikes beer, the beer's isohumulones—chemicals released when hops boil—break down, creating chemical compounds identical to those found in skunk spray. Never buy bottled beer shelved in a window.

Sparging Removing the grains from the mash, leaving behind hot, watery wort.

Standard reference method (SRM) The system that measures beer color. See pages 260–261.

Triple IPA A huge IPA heaped with hops. No hard-and-fast definition applies, but a good rule of thumb is that triples start at 10% ABV.

Wet-hop beer A delicate, ephemeral fall specialty made with just-harvested hops not kilned or dried. It typically releases in September and October. See *fresh-hop beer.*

Wheat Cereal grain that contributes smooth character, hazy hue, and light tartness to beer.

Whirlpool Technique for collecting clumped tannins and protein by creating a vortex. (Homebrewers stir wort with a spoon.) Hops introduced during this process largely impart aroma and flavor rather than bitterness.

Wild ale A catchall category of funky-tasting, offbeat beers dosed with wild yeast such as *Brettanomyces* and perhaps souring bacteria, including *Lactobacillus* or *Pediococcus.*

Wort The hot soup extracted from the mash. It's an all-you-can-eat buffet for the yeast that creates beer.

Yeast The microscopic critters that create alcohol and make beer o'clock the best time of day. Each strain provides a different flavor profile.

SRM COLOR CHART

The Standard Reference Method measures the color of beer. It represents the absorption of one point of light through beer, so it doesn't take into account the red of a kriek or framboise, for example, but it does offer an objective scale against which to check the color of your brew.

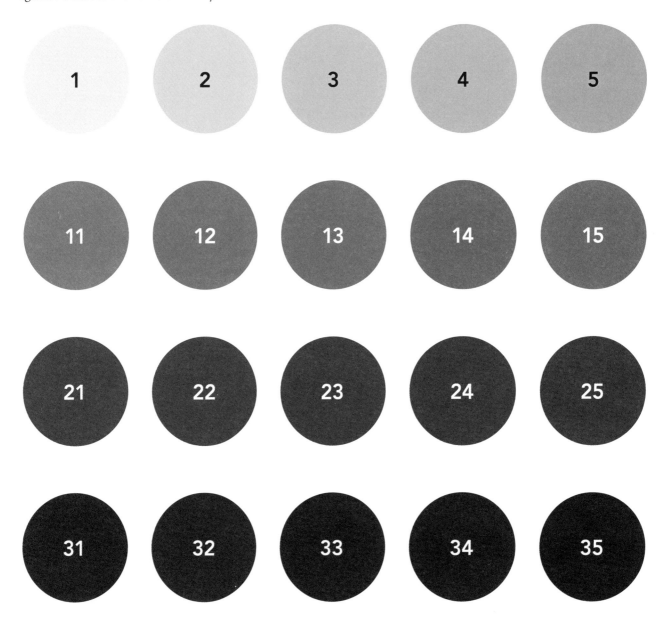

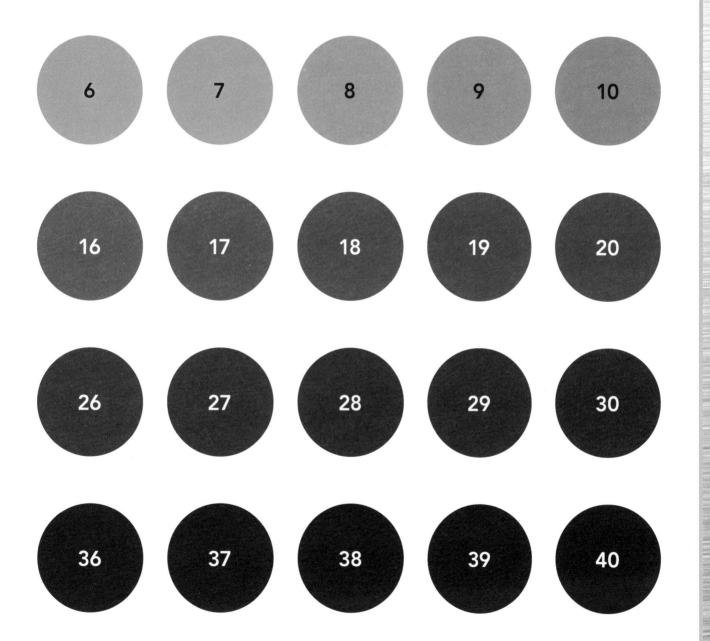

ACKNOWLEDGMENTS

How did I find the homebrewers in this book? Instead of typing "homebrewer" into Google and praying to the algorithm gods to deliver search-engine gold, I mined pretty much every beer-industry contact in my address book and ever so politely asked for help. A million billion thanks to Joe Stange, Stan Hieronymus, Matt Curtis, Joe Wiebe, Rory Lawton, Blake Stone-Banks, Carl Setzer, Brian Devine, Maree Shaw, Lee Reeve, Sigurdur Snorrason, John Preston, Mike Leupold, Lucy Corne, Nina Anika Klotz, Nora McGunnigle, Derek Walsh, and Ken Getty. You all have earned that next round.

John LaPolla and Douglas Amport deserve a round of applause for making sure the recipes are shipshape. Visit their homebrew shop, Bitter & Esters, next time you're in Brooklyn.

Huge thanks to Team Sterling Publishing for turning this collection of vowels, consonants, and images into, you know, a book. Take a bow and a beer from the cooler, James Jayo, Stacey Stambaugh, Christine Heun, Igor Satanovsky, Scott Amerman, and Ben Brandstein.

Last but not least, a massive thanks to all the homebrewers who graciously shared their time, stories, and tasty recipes. May all your fermentations be fruitful.

IMAGE CREDITS

The author and publisher thank all of the brewers and individuals who provided images for use in this book.

Cover: **iStock**: © Alina_Fedorova: bottle illustrations; © **Matt Neilson**: back cover photo; **Shutterstock.com**: Jesus Cervantes: wood grain; paseven: brewing illustration; Tashal: beer cap

All images courtesy of the corresponding brewers with the following additions: **Alamy**: Dorothy Alexander: 56; Vladislav Sernov: 235; © **Alberto Alcocer**: 46, 47, 48–49, 50, 52, 53; © Aaron Andujar: 223, 224, 227, 228, 229; © **BC Ale Trail/Destination BC**: 151; © **Adam Beauchamp**: 103; © Joshua M. Bernstein: VIX, 106; © **Bootleg Biology**: Laurel Staples: 184, 185, 186, 187, 189; © **Bright Wave Media**: 135, 136; © **Bryce Boyer**: 236, 237; **Courtesy CHAOS Brew Club**: 105; © **Emma Christensen**: 115, 117; © **Simon Clippingdale**: 140–141; © **Juren David**: 216–217; © **Thomas De Cian**: 245, 246; © **Ramiro De Diego**: 128, 129, 130, 131; **Courtesy Brian Devine**: 205, 207; © **Marco Fugallo**: 240; © **Matt Furman Photography**: 210, 212, 214–215, 257, 263; Getty Images: © Walter Bibikow: 180; © Tony Briscoe/Dorling Kindersley: 45; © Danita Delimont: 192–193; © Eric Futran-Chefshots: XVI; © Russell Hart: 209; **iStock**: © AsianDream: 122; © bhofack2: 7, 95, 133; © cegli: 96; © Denis: spotlight; © Detanan: 125; © Alina Fedorova: bottle illustrations; © GoodLifeStudio:

35; © Eddie Hernandez Photography: 253; © Ina Peters: 23; © inese online: 79; © ISMODE: grunge texture; © Ken Rygh: X; © kokoroyuki: aluminum; © Magone: 139; © novaaleksandra: graph paper; © rasilja: XV; © Luerat Satichob: beer icons; © wundervisuals: 161; © zimmytws: 219; © zmurciuk_k: 29; **Mary's Selfie Stick**: 211; © **Katrina Matthews/ Zoiglhaus Brewing Company**: 111, 112–113; © **Matt Neilson**: 155, 156–157, 159; © **2015 Katie Newburn**: from BREW BETTER BEER: LEARN (AND BREAK) THE RULES FOR MAKING IPAS, SOURS, PILSNERS, STOUTS, AND MORE by EMMA Christensen. Used by permission of Ten Speed Press, an imprint of the Crown Publishing Group, a division of Penguin Random House LLC. All rights reserved: 119; © **Hörður Ellert Ólafsson**: 239; © **Nigel Robb**: 36, 37, 38–39, 41, 42–43; **Glen Alvarez Rodríguez**: 199, 200, 203; © **John Schulz Photography**: 127; **Shutterstock.com**: Alp Aksoy: 243; Jesus Cervantes: wood grain; DOPhoto: 55; Suriel Ramzal: 57; symbiot: 171; © **Yannick So**: 250; © **southstreetco.com**: 165, 166–167, 169; © **Brian Spencer**: 244; © **Tim Stahl**: XII–XIII, 8, 9, 10–11, 12, 14–15, 17, 100–101, 254; **Stocksy United**: © Bonninstudio: 271; © Andrew Cebulka: 85; © Jill Chen: 75, 249; © Suzanne Clements: 162, 196; © Kristin Duvall: 149; © Raymond Forbes: 63; © Gillian van Niekerk : 99; © Tana Teel: 61; © Victor Torre: 262; © Jeff Wasserman: 69, 109, 177; © Cameron Whitman: 183; © **Scott Van Campen**: 83; © **Nathalie Van de Walle**: 65, 66, 67; © **Lea Woodard**: 179

INDEX

(continued)

ABOUT THE AUTHOR

Joshua M. Bernstein is a beer, spirits, food, and travel journalist and the author of *Brewed Awakening, The Complete Beer Course,* and *Complete IPA* (Sterling Epicure). His work appears regularly in newspapers, magazines, and websites, including *The New York Times, Men's Journal, Wine Enthusiast, BeerAdvocate, Draft, Bon Appétit, New York, Saveur,* and *Imbibe,* where he oversees beer coverage as contributing editor. Beer Sessions Radio, CNBC, Fox Business, and NPR's *Marketplace* have featured him as a beer expert, and he consults for breweries, bars, and bottle shops and leads private tasting seminars and tours. He lives with his wife and daughter in Brooklyn.

Photo by Tod Seele